The Competent Head

The Competent Head
A Job Analysis of Heads' Tasks and Personality Factors

Dilum Jirasinghe
Geoffrey Lyons

 The Falmer Press

(A member of the Taylor & Francis Group)
London • Washington, D.C.

UK   Falmer Press, 1 Gunpowder Square, London, EC4A 3DE
USA   Falmer Press, Taylor and Francis Inc., 1900 Frost Road, Suite 101, Bristol, PA 19007

First published in 1996

A catalogue record for this book is available from the British Library

Library of Congress Cataloging-in-Publication Data are available on request

ISBN 0 7507 0522 1 cased
ISBN 0 7507 0523 X paper

Jacket design by Caroline Archer

Typeset in 10/12pt Times by
Graphicraft Typesetters Ltd., Hong Kong.

Printed in Great Britain by Biddles Ltd., Guildford and King's Lynn on paper which has a specified pH value on final paper manufacture of not less than 7.5 and is therefore 'acid free'.

Contents

Contents

List of Tables and Figures

Acknowledgments

Times of great change in education may in retrospect prove to have been challenging and exciting but without doubt place an unrelenting workload on those directly involved. At such a time that so many heads, LEA inspectors and officers were willing to participate in this phase of the research project is a tribute to their belief in the continued development of the profession. The authors therefore wish to acknowledge their thanks to all those LEAs that helped with the research particularly Barnet, Brent, Calderdale, Camden, Coventry, Cumbria, Essex, Greenwich, Gwent, Herefordshire, Kirklees, Mid Glamorgan, Newham and Northumberland, and gave such commitment.

Many others have helped. Colleagues of the University of East London gave us the initial encouragement, sustained the project and enabled this phase of the research to reach a successful outcome. Harold Heller helped the project get into the field. Christopher Davies, Mark Fox, Roy Griffiths, Richard Meredith and Marlene Rowbotham commented on materials and the emerging drafts of the manuscript.

Throughout the project Bob Parkinson, David Erlandson and Lloyd McCleary have been constant and freely available sources of insight, practical help and theoretical advice, ideas and encouragement. Our work has been much improved by their constructive comments.

The authors freely acknowledge their debt to Saville and Holdsworth Ltd, whose instruments were used in the research, particularly to James Bywater and Sara Worth. Throughout, Saville and Holdsworth Ltd have underpinned our work and by making available to us their experience have proved an ever-ready source of ideas, expertise, help and encouragement.

The opinions and ideas expressed here are those of the authors, however, and we accept responsibility for them.

Dilum Jirasinghe
Geoffrey Lyons
East London Business School
University of East London

Abbreviations Used

AMA   American Management Association
IT   information technology
LEA   local education authority
LMS   local management of schools
MBTI   Myers-Briggs Type Inventory
MCI   Management Charter Initiative
NASSP   National Association of Secondary School Principals
NCVQ   National Council for Vocational Qualifications
NEAC   National Educational Assessment Centre
NFMED   National Forum for Management Education and Development
NVQ   National Vocational Qualification
OFSTED   Office for Standards in Education
OPQ   Occupational Personality Questionnaire
SATS   Standard Achievement Tests for Schools
SHL   Saville and Holdsworth Limited
16PF   16 Personality Factor
SMS   School Management South
STEN   standard ten
TEED   Training Enterprise and Education Department
TTA   Teacher Training Agency
WPS   Work Profiling System

Introduction

I

It is widely accepted that educational institutions in order to be effective require effective leaders. Objective and rigorous assessment criteria by which such leaders may be assessed have however hitherto proved elusive and difficult to obtain.

This book sets out to provide a basis by which the assessment of education leaders can take place, by describing the process in generating and validating more objective and accurate assessment criteria. This is particularly pertinent at the present time in fully meeting equal opportunity concerns.

The approach adopted is applicable across the education sectors. The discussion here is however focused upon the position of headteachers of maintained schools.

The authors put forward the case that in order to make objective assessment decisions it is necessary first, that an accurate current description of the head's job is available, and that, in order to provide assessable and replicable data, this should be achieved through a process of job analysis. Second, the data derived from a systematically conducted job analysis should then be used to generate and validate management competencies accurately reflecting the head's responsibilities. Management competencies then in turn provide the criteria for assessment decision making. The competencies which we propose are used for headship positions are those competencies normally described as 'personal' and 'transferable'.

The techniques of job analysis and the generation and use of management competencies have long been widely used in non-educational employment sectors. The authors advocate their use in education, not assuming that schools and colleges are businesses or should be treated as if they were businesses, but with respect to jobs and the selection of staff, schools have much in common with organizations in non-educational employment sectors.

The book is principally directed towards scholars, practice orientated researchers and practitioners in education, particularly those practitioners undertaking award bearing programmes of study. The busy practitioner, while interested in the practical outcomes to the report of the data collection and analysis, may well wish to omit the theory related chapters from their use of the book.

II

Unprecedented change since the late 1980s to the present day has been imposed upon the maintained school sector in the UK largely by government. It is intended to make the system more accountable, open and responsive to the local community, including employers, and to be more demonstrably cost effective. The measures have included: the imposition of a national curriculum; testing of pupils at key stages of their education and the publication of school results as league tables; a locally managed school budget; a parents' charter and parental choice of school; competition between schools for pupils; new and increased powers for school governors, including responsibility for assessment decision making; staff appraisal; compulsory inspection for schools, and the publication of an inspection report. These are indicative of the many initiatives now being implemented. Educational change is with us and will continue into the future. Within this context the job of the head who leads the school has altered and headship itself is undergoing a fundamental transformation.

Accordingly, the need to identify and to train headteachers to perform a more complex job is more crucial than was previously the case. In order for this to occur it is necessary to have an accurate, objective, and comprehensive view of the head's job now. The magnitude of changes to the school system indicate in the authors' opinion that a fresh approach be adopted, and one that is easily replicable and easily updated.

The principal technique employed in the study reported here is that of job analysis. It is used in non-educational employment sectors but not used systematically within education and with schools in the maintained sector in particular.

Job analysis is a process capable of producing outcomes of practical relevance to heads and other senior staff in schools, and to governors and trainers. It is also a methodology for applied research. The sophistication of the techniques and analysis utilized enables a picture of the head to be drawn which has a high degree of reliability and validity. Further, it enables assessment criteria, that is management competencies, to be identified and assessment materials and follow-on training to be developed. In addition, the replicability of the process permits continuity of use in one setting and transferability to other settings. Within this context some steps can be taken towards examining the relationship between criteria identified and successful job performance.

Many studies of the work of headteachers in the UK have been conducted using a variety of approaches and focusing upon various aspects of the role, similarly studies have been conducted of the school leader position in other countries (e.g. Wolcott 1973; Lyons 1974, 1976; McCleary et al. 1978; Webb and Lyons 1982; Clerkin 1985; Jenkins 1985; Morgan et al. 1983; Jones 1987; Mortimore et al. 1988; Nias et al. 1989; Erlandson et al. 1990; Audit Commission 1991; Ribbins 1994; Thomas and Bullock 1994).

The works cited above focus attention upon certain underlying problems relating to studies of occupational roles. These include: (1) data collection and analysis and (2) comparison of findings across settings in a single occupation, across occupational sectors, or between countries. The work reported here provides new insights to these problems.

Currently much research and interest in education management concerns school effectiveness. One of the major factors contributing to school effectiveness is of course the effectiveness of the head. The research reported here examines headteacher effectiveness from a different standpoint to that usually adopted in the education literature cited above. The approach is a fresh one that generates and uses headteacher management competencies to underpin the assessment of headteacher effectiveness.

Competencies are put forward here as an insightful approach for first, describing the skills and qualities associated with effective headship, and second, enabling an objective and accurate assessment to be made of a head's job performance. The latter is crucial in underpinning improved selection and recruitment, development and training of heads.

The need for the assessment process to be open and impartial, and fully meet the demands of equal opportunity legislation and policies is self-evident, and certainly so in our multiethnic society, and when gender bias in appointments to headship are apparently occurring on a regional basis (see Edwards and Lyons 1994).

We propose an incremental stepping stone approach to lay down a basis upon which future frameworks can be developed. In such circumstances it is essential that data produced is examined against the stringency of field considerations, before the next step is taken. We believe that this approach towards understanding headteacher effectiveness can make a significant contribution to the school effectiveness movement. We are of the opinion that the techniques advanced here produce a rich source of data which can lead to criteria and techniques that make the assessment process more rational and objective than might otherwise be the case. The interest here is to demonstrate the utility of the approach to the education sector and present some practical outcomes. The work is the beginning of a lengthy process which will build incrementally.

This book is directed towards

- those involved in the process of headteacher recruitment and selection, and
- those involved in headteacher management development, both diagnostic and training aspects, and including short course and award bearing programmes as well as programmes of self-directed study.

The above include: governors, inspectors, consultants, trainers, LEA inspectors and education officers, as well as those individuals in higher education institutions who provide courses and training.

Self-evidently, the book is of interest to

- serving headteachers, deputy heads, and other members of senior staff in schools; and
- those undertaking research degrees, and to active practice orientated researchers in the UK and in other countries.

A national research project has been conducted to undertake a job analysis of heads at a time of significant change. This has involved at various stages over 280 headteachers (although for analysis purposes the sample was confined to 255 heads).

Headteachers were drawn from across England and Wales, and represented various types of schools, phases of education and experience of headship. Additionally, smaller numbers of inspectors, advisers, education officers as well as deputy heads were involved in the later stages of the research. The data collected enabled us to determine heads' tasks and the contexts in which job tasks are performed, and heads' preferred personality dimensions and styles. This data, supplemented by intensive interviewing, was then used to generate and validate management competencies for heads.

The research has been undertaken throughout in collaboration with a major firm of occupational psychology management consultants in the UK, Saville and Holdsworth Ltd, whose instruments were utilized in the research.

III

The book is divided into three interlinking parts: the underpinning theoretical rationale and framework; the findings of a national research project concerning headteachers; and the practical outcomes of relevance to assessing and developing headteachers. Each part is described in greater detail below and the parts may well be of different interest to the readership. While the book is constructed to have an internal coherence and development, it may prove that different readers choose to read the book in whichever sequence is of most use and interest to them. Those who wish to omit the theoretical chapters on job analysis and competencies can proceed to the findings of the field research. However, they will need to accept on trust our analysis and recommendations.

Part 1 presents a theoretical underpinning, and is conceived for those who have more time for reflection, or wish to add theoretical substance to their knowledge before accepting the techniques proposed here for adoption within the schools sector. It comprises Chapter 1, an examination of job analysis; and Chapter 2, an examination of the theoretical issues underpinning the generation and use of management competencies.

Chapter 1 includes a description of the main job analysis approaches, its application to the schools sector, and a consideration of the practical aspects of conducting a study. There is a review of some job analysis techniques and a discussion of underlying issues in the application of systematic job analysis to the position of headteacher.

Chapter 2 first considers what a competence based approach can offer to education management. It is then divided into three sections:

- 'a framework for conceptualizing competence', drawing together the two major approaches to the generation and use of competencies into a unifying framework, as well as considering criticisms of competency-based approaches;
- 'selecting a suitable approach to competence', views the two approaches to competence as complementary, and includes a review of some factors to be considered in choosing an appropriate approach. There is also a discussion

on deriving competencies, the use of 'generic' competencies, as well as competencies which are specific to the occupation, the organization, and the individual;

- 'measuring and assessing an individual's competence', comprising a selected review of competence assessment methods; a focus on issues underlying competence assessment such as its relationship with performance; and the place of knowledge and understanding, and the influence of time.

Part 2 of the book presents the findings of the field research. It comprises Chapter 3 and includes:

- the findings of a self-report 'occupational based personality questionnaire', which compares heads against the norm for managers and other professional workers in the UK. It examines some of the differences occurring between heads' responses, particularly those related to gender. Heads' preferred leadership styles and team types are also identified;
- the results of a job analysis questionnaire relating to: categories of job tasks, specific tasks, context factors, and time management issues;
- the results of the two questionnaire approaches, used to present a headteacher's profile, comprising job description and person specification; and
- a discussion of some of the dilemmas and problems of headship which the research has so far identified and which necessarily must be confronted by practising heads and those involved in headteacher assessment.

Part 3 of the book, which contains Chapters 4 and 5, focuses on the practical outcomes of the research as they relate to assessing and developing headteachers. A competency model of headteachers and the practical use of competencies to benefit heads are presented.

Chapter 4 initially describes the stages in deriving and validating a set of competencies for heads. The headteacher management competencies derived from the research are presented, and this framework is compared to other headteacher competence models, and also to generic models for use with all managers. The chapter concludes with a discussion of the problematic issues of establishing predictive validity, and headteacher and school effectiveness.

Chapter 5 examines indicative ways in which objective 'competency' led headteacher assessment might take place to underpin recruitment and selection, management development and training, and appraisal. A number of competence assessment techniques are highlighted, particularly the assessment centre process, and self-evaluation. A simple indicative self-evaluation document for heads is included in this chapter. Finally there is a focus on the use of a '360 degree approach' to assessing and developing heads, as well as the use of mentoring partnerships to support heads.

The concluding section to the book provides a summary of the main issues raised, identifies some of the problems which are beginning to emerge and indicates a future research agenda.

Part I

Rationale and Framework

The imposition of new tasks and responsibilities upon those who lead schools has been such that in order to deal effectively with current reforms it is necessary that school leaders develop and use a range of managerial skills and behaviours. The latter may be far removed from those headteacher attributes and skills which have emerged from much previous research into school management, e.g. the head's functions polarized into professional and administrative leadership.

The job of headteacher is changing significantly. In these circumstances it is appropriate to provide an accurate description of the behaviours and attributes underpinning headship at the present time. Thus approaches to training, management development, selection and recruitment of headteachers may need to be recast, first to be of support to headteachers at the present time, and second to be more accurate, objective and lead to successful long term outcomes.

Management competencies are put forward in this book as an approach to describe those behaviours and attributes comprising effective headship. Such competencies can be objectively assessed, enabling an accurate evaluation of a headteacher's current or potential job performance and prove crucial in underpinning management development, training, selection and recruitment.

New and different tools and techniques will be needed to identify accurately the 'emerging' competencies underpinning job performance at the current time. In selecting a methodology which is sufficiently sophisticated to identify the competencies, and in ensuring that the technique is replicable for others to emulate, a systematic process known as job analysis is adopted here.

Job analysis is widely used in non-educational employment sectors as important to a greater understanding of managerial jobs. It has not previously been used in such a consistent manner, and with such a large sample, with headteachers as in this book.

Part I of the book examines what job analysis and a competence-based approach can offer education management, and explores the underpinning rationale and framework behind each of these concepts. Part I is in two chapters. Chapter 1 reviews job analysis, while Chapter 2 discusses the major issues surrounding management competencies: conceptualizing competence, selection of a suitable approach to competence, and measuring and assessing competence. Those who at this stage do not require the detail of the theoretical underpinning to the approaches treated here, should move to Chapter 3 where the research data gathered by job analysis is reported.

Chapter 1

Job Analysis

Introduction

This chapter describes and discusses job analysis and its relevance for today's managers in the education sector. It offers practical advice on the conduct of job analysis; sets out the advantages and disadvantages of some job analysis techniques; and discusses some underlying issues of the job analysis process.

What is Job Analysis?

Job analysis is a systematic process for acquiring objective and detailed information about jobs. It is not a single methodology but a generic term representing a range of techniques. The data gathered may be in the form of information on job tasks, roles, and job holder attributes relevant to job performance. Material collected can relate to the job currently being performed or directed at a job which is likely to be performed in the near future.

Job analysis is carefully structured although the extent of structure will vary according to the different techniques available. The process is analytical, and breaks down the job into its component parts, rather than describing the job as a whole (Saville and Holdsworth 1995).

Job analysis is designed to achieve a specific goal(s), and is typically in the form of the 'what' – tasks and activities which are associated with the job; the 'how' – the skills and abilities required to perform these tasks; and the 'context' – the environment or culture in which tasks are executed. For example the job analysis of headteachers (described in detail in Chapter 3) identifies the major job tasks of heads – planning, motivating, implementing/coordinating, etc.; derives the skills and abilities critical to successful job performance such as confidence, the need to be sympathetic and tolerant, to be consultative, etc.; and constructs a picture of the context in which the head undertakes his/her work, including his/her freedom to structure the job, the number of staff in school, working hours and so forth.

Job analysis can be viewed not only as a process capable of producing a number of practical outcomes of benefit to practitioners, trainers and the like, but also as an applied form of research (Pearn and Kandola 1988). The job analyst gathers pertinent data in a systematic and reliable manner in the identification, resolution, or redefinition of a problem or in addressing a specific need. For example, the job analysis of heads undertaken here has enabled us to derive up-to-date job relevant criteria to underpin improved and more objective selection and recruitment of headteachers.

Job Analysis and Its Application to the School Sector

Schools and in particular headteachers, as they face the challenges of today's changing competitive world with its new technology, have to adopt new roles and ways of working. For example, in the UK there is a move towards greater accountability and increased responsibility of governors, a four year inspection cycle, and responsibility for the school's financial management, which have presented new, challenging demands to headteachers. It is therefore timely to redefine tasks, objectives and responsibilities for those who work in schools, and have clear and easily accessible information about jobs and the human characteristics required to perform job tasks.

It is argued in this chapter that job analysis based on evidence is more appropriate than speculation or reliance on informal procedures which may have previously been successful (Pearn and Kandola 1988). Processes linked with job analysis and those employed in the present research are objective, rigorous and utilize tools and techniques of proven validity and reliability to ensure accurate identification of job information.

The importance of rigorous and detailed job analysis in underpinning human resource development and in sustaining an integrated approach to human resource management in schools cannot be overestimated. Recruitment and selection procedures, training needs analysis, and appraisal procedures etc., are all likely to benefit from job or competency definitions which are produced directly from an analysis of job behaviours. As a result procedures for recruitment and selection, etc. are likely to be more accurate and less susceptible to bias and distortion than some other previously utilized techniques, for example, the traditional interview process relying on instinctive criteria or a 'gut feeling'.

Employment and equal opportunities legislation are additional factors supporting the application of the job analysis process to schools. There is a requirement to safeguard job applicants and employees from discrimination due to race, gender or disability. In the case of a school, for example, asked to justify the criteria used in selection, the systematic use of evidence collected through a rigorous and accurate job analysis is likely to represent the best means of defence from legal scrutiny, as well as the desire to deal with people in an ethically accepted way.

Employing procedures of proven precision and validity is likely to enhance job holders' satisfactions and perceptions of assessment processes, be they for selection or development purposes. This may prove vital in gaining willing participation and cooperation of school staff.

Three Approaches to Job Analysis

It is generally accepted in the work relating to job analysis that it can be broadly divided into three different types of approaches, each with its own supporting techniques. These are: task or job orientated approaches, behaviour or job holder methods, and attribute or trait strategies (McCormick 1976). The purpose of the section that now follows is to describe them and show their usefulness to school management.

The first of these, task or job orientated job analysis, describes work in terms of outcomes or tasks completed (e.g. produce annual budget; formulate school development plan). The work of the UK Management Charter Initiative (MCI) in producing nationally recognized 'standards' of performance for managers, and of the National Council for Vocational Qualifications (NCVQ) in producing National Vocational Qualifications (NVQs) exemplifies the adoption of such a job analysis approach (see Chapter 2). To do this, the MCI and the NCVQ have employed the technique of functional analysis which is discussed in Chapter 2.

The most common tools by which the description is achieved however are task inventories or checklists. The task descriptions derived from these tend to be specific to a particular job and the technology currently in use. The approach, while capable of giving a very detailed and specific description of a job, is limited in its ability to identify common elements across jobs. For example, many of the job descriptions to be found in earlier school handbooks suffered from similar limitations.

The converse is true of behaviour or job holder orientated job analysis techniques, which describe work in terms of more generalized behaviours or activities (e.g. analyzing numerical data, making decisions after evaluation, encouraging cooperation). This method produces information about the job which is less specific, but behaviours generated are common to a much wider range of jobs enabling similarities and differences to be identified. The information generated is likely to be more useful than checklists for training and management development, particularly in identifying those elements of the job which are transferable, for example, across school sectors, and possibly even across occupational domains. For schools this might for example include elements such as planning long term and short term objectives; creating a good team spirit; formulating or adjusting policy due to change. The approach focuses on what the job holder does rather than the specific job outcomes to be achieved, and is therefore also referred to as 'job holder orientated'.

Finally attribute or trait orientated job analysis techniques depict jobs in terms of the human attributes, i.e. abilities, personality characteristics etc., that are required to perform work activities (e.g. self-confidence, creativity, numerical reasoning). The major advantage of this approach is that it collects and presents job information in a manner which is directly amenable for use in assessment procedures such as selection, appraisal, and management development. The problem with this approach, however, is that in practice it is difficult to move directly from an analysis of job content to the corresponding human attributes necessary for job performance.

For schools, while the approach to job analysis adopted is likely to be contingent upon the purpose of the job analysis and the particular position under study, the authors would advocate a two stage process: first, to arrive at a description of the job in terms of tasks and/or behaviours, and second, to use this description to identify the underlying attributes or 'competencies' that underpin and give rise to these tasks and behaviours.

Practical Issues to Consider

The authors, based on their experience, suggest that there are a number of practical issues to be considered in conducting a job analysis which should prove helpful for those readers who wish to examine the possibilities:

- selection of an appropriate job analysis technique. The choice of method should be led by the purpose of the job analysis investigation. A clear vision of the end point is essential in guiding the selection of a suitable method, in ensuring objectives are met, and in making sure the analysis stays on course. It is also important from the experience of the authors to ensure that all elements of the job are covered, e.g. task identification, frequency of occurrence and time spent on tasks, prioritization of tasks, and job context factors. These all interact to determine the necessary human attributes in describing effective performance;
- the job under study will make some job analysis methods more preferable to others. For example, in some jobs key elements – such as problem solving or decision making – may not be amenable to direct observation methods, the duties of senior management being a case in point. In such a case, a structured job analysis questionnaire or job analysis interview would seem to be more appropriate;
- access factors, i.e. ease of access to job holders, their superordinates and subordinates;
- resourcing and timescale issues;
- expertise of job analysts; some job analysis techniques require training before use;
- availability and acquiescence of job holders to fully cooperate in the process, for example by clearly communicating that the job analysis is not linked with appraisal;
- whether to focus on job holders not differentiated in terms of ability, or to focus on 'superior' or upon 'average' job performers;
- ethical considerations;
- political considerations, which may include: reassurance as to the purpose of the analysis, and the involvement in the job analysis as far as practicable of individuals interacting with the job holder at all levels;
- the quality of the information obtained is also a primary consideration in selecting job interviewees; for example, job holders should generally be experienced individuals and superordinates should be experienced, discerning, and forward looking;
- other factors will also guide the choice of job analysis interviewees, for example, in reflecting the diversity of the workforce by adequately representing women, ethnic minorities, age groups etc., and in securing a sample of the range of task variation within the job;
- in assembling a comprehensive picture of a job, two or more job analysis techniques will be necessary. This is particularly important as no one single

method is likely to be capable of providing the detail, breadth, and depth that is crucial in ensuring that all relevant information about the job is collected;
- best practice would dictate a team of job analysts collaborating on any one job analysis, in this way ensuring that objectivity and standards are consistently at a premium.

In practice we recognize that it may be difficult for schools in conducting a job analysis to meet all the above requirements. We would therefore suggest that they examine the information presented in Chapter 3 in the form of a job description and person specification for heads or refer to the competencies identified in Chapter 4, to determine the extent to which these meet the school's requirements. If this is not the case, schools may wish to undertake some supplementary data collection by simple questionnaire, or structured interview, to job holders and/or their superordinates.

The principal features of job analysis, including the three main approaches, and the potential benefits to be derived from the application of the job analysis process to the schools sector have been described. A number of important practicalities to be considered prior to conducting a job analysis have also been offered. The next section reviews some job analysis techniques, their major characteristics, and identifies the advantages and disadvantages associated with each technique.

A Review of Some Job Analysis Techniques

The reader will be conversant with some job analysis techniques used in a schools context, for example, the use of interviews; observational techniques; and diaries or time-logs. (For reviews of job analysis and associated techniques consult Levine *et al.* 1983; Gael 1983, 1987; Ghorpade 1988; and Pearn and Kandola 1993.) In the present research with headteachers it was necessary, because of the senior management responsibility of the post holder, to adopt a task and behavioural approach to analyzing the job.

After considering a range of job analysis techniques, it was decided that the following methods were the most suitable in satisfying the research requirements. The job analysis techniques advocated here are: the Work Profiling System, the Occupational Personality Questionnaire;[1] critical incidents analysis and repertory grids analysis. The techniques selected had the capacity to generate varied and usable outcomes; were appropriate for use with senior management roles; and included techniques which were structured and standardized for use with large samples, as well as more unstructured methods capable of identifying subtle aspects of the job. Each of these methods is described in turn below.

The Work Profiling System (WPS)

The Work Profiling System (WPS), developed in 1989 by Saville and Holdsworth Ltd is an 'integrated' job analysis system. It may be viewed as producing data which is both 'task/job' orientated and 'job holder/behaviour' orientated. Information is collected about a job in a structured manner and computer analyzed in order to meet a variety of objectives; including, the specification of job tasks and job context, profiling of human attributes required for effective job performance, and the identification of relevant assessment methods. For example, a job description and person specification for headteachers is presented in Chapter 3.

Administration is through a questionnaire, and can be supplemented with 'validation' interviews conducted by the job analyst where the respondent is questioned about his/her responses. There are three versions of the questionnaire covering different jobs across occupational areas: technical/manual, service/administrative, and managerial/professional. All three versions of the questionnaire could be used in schools. The research reported here has utilized the managerial/professional version, the findings of which are presented in Chapter 3.

The questionnaire has the advantage of being suitable for a variety of purposes, to be used on a one-to-one basis or with large groups of job holders. It is highly structured and sophisticated with rapid questionnaire administration and analysis. The structured nature of the questionnaire may however entail that it is supplemented with other job analysis technique(s), where necessary, allowing respondents to add pertinent 'extra' information.

Critical Incidents

Critical incidents analysis – pioneered by J.C. Flanagan in the 1950s (Flanagan 1954) – is a procedure for collecting observed 'incidents' which have proved very important or critical to job performance. Incidents may be obtained illustrating both positive and negative performance. The incidents, usually collected in a one-to-one interview with job holders (or superordinates), are recorded in the form of notes, stories or anecdotes.

A typical critical incidents procedure might proceed as follows (Saville and Holdsworth 1990c):

- statement of the method and its objectives by the interviewer;
- the identification of job objectives by job holder;
- preparation of notes on incident by respondent;
- relating and noting incident; and
- hypothesis formation.

The last stage in this process involves both the interviewer and the job holder discussing the skills, abilities etc. highlighted in the incident. Critical incidents analysis can be used on large samples using quantitative data analysis, but in the authors' experience the technique is a rich source of qualitative information based on a relatively small sample. In this context it may be useful for schools as a job analysis technique which is also flexible and relatively easy to use with minimal training.

The recall of incidents relies on individuals' memories and may tend to illustrate positive, rather than negative, job performance. The anecdotal style of the method, however, can be invaluable in bringing colour and richness to a job analysis which may otherwise be rather mundane and lifeless. The technique also provides information which distinguishes effective from less effective job performance.

Repertory Grid

The technique has been developed from the personal construct theory of George Kelly (Kelly 1955). In its use in job analysis, the objective is to map out an individual's 'constructs' (i.e. perceptions or views) of the job in question through a one-to-one interview.

This is achieved by generating a 'grid' of the individual's thoughts or constructs about elements in the job. In a job analysis context, the 'elements' are usually job holders. By specifying as elements both successful job performers and less successful job performers, the technique can be used to identify the constructs which discriminate between these two groups. A process of 'laddering' (i.e. in-depth probing) also enables behavioural indicators to be identified for each construct. Repertory grids analysis is particularly useful when used to interview superordinates. For example, in the present research inspectors/advisers were asked to identify critical factors which they felt differentiated effective from less effective headteacher performance.

The technique can elicit a large amount of rich data and is particularly pertinent in obtaining knowledge of job facets difficult to observe directly. In conducting repertory grid interviews the authors would recommend selecting as interviewees those superordinates and/or job holders with the capacity to be insightful and analytical regarding the job.

The Occupational Personality Questionnaire

An examination of the criteria and results of many job analysis projects suggests that up to 70 per cent of the attributes which are associated with success at work are dimensions of personality rather than ability (Saville and Holdsworth 1990a). Examples of personality questionnaires regularly used in occupational contexts include the Occupational Personality Questionnaire (OPQ), the Myers-Briggs Type Inventory (MBTI), and the 16 Personality Factor (16PF) Questionnaire. Many of these questionnaires were however designed for use with clinical populations. The Occupational Personality Questionnaire (OPQ) has the advantage of being designed solely for occupational use, and has therefore been used in the present research.

Generally personality questionnaires are not used as part of the job analysis process, because they describe individual preferences in terms of work behaviour, and represent aspects of the person rather than aspects of the job. Exceptionally, the sampling of a large number of job incumbents, and the production of significant numbers of job holders' occupational personality profiles, may serve to identify those personality attributes underlying task performance which seem to be common across job holders. It is possible in this way to speculate on behaviours, leadership styles etc., which appear to be representative of the job or occupation.

There is a danger that results may reflect peculiarities/idiosyncrasies of a particular sample population rather than identify factors associated with job performance. The Occupational Personality Questionnaire is however likely to identify aspects of the job not captured by other job analysis techniques, for example attributes and leadership styles. In our experience individual profiles produced by the Occupational Personality Questionnaire are also of considerable interest to job holders, for example, for reflection and self-evaluation.

Underlying Issues in the Application of a Systematic Job Analysis to the Position of Headteacher

The previous section has reviewed a number of job analysis techniques. This review has highlighted the various methodologies at an operational level, but several other underlying issues of the job analysis process itself are worth examination.

The job analysis may be guided towards a specific outcome by adoption of a strategy which is value-driven rather than objective, for example for schools attempting a cultural transformation. The adoption of an impartial approach to analyzing the head's job may reinforce the status quo, and is acceptable for occupational positions which are relatively stable. For jobs undergoing fundamental change however (particularly where change is externally imposed) job holders themselves may still be adjusting to the consequences of ongoing reforms. Thus the views of 'significant others', for example experienced inspectors/advisers/education officers/governors, are also required to envision the future job role. One of the essential considerations here is whether the head's job is to be analyzed as it is currently performed, or as it should be performed.

There are problems in obtaining useful data (Pearn and Kandola 1993): a 'snapshot' of the job at a specific point in time gives little insight into how the job will evolve in the future; a job takes on different properties depending on who is performing the work, although this may be context related; and there are 'situation-determined changes' influenced by the context/environment in which the job is located. These problems will affect the reliability of the analysis conducted on heads.

The reduction of the headteacher's job into its finite task or behavioural elements is another underlying issue. There is a danger that in the process, the coherence of the job as a whole, which lies in interrelating behaviours and tasks, may be missed by job analysts.

Allied to this, job analysis as a process may artificially distort the job under study. For example, heightened awareness by heads may influence their job performance either through an increase in anxiety resulting in errors otherwise absent, or a desire to portray the job/performance at its best, although the authors' experience would suggest that such influences are small.

A further issue is raised by Saville and Holdsworth (1995) who assert that the role of the job analyst is easily taken for granted and this can lead to problems. They state that job analysts should be properly trained; have a working knowledge of the organization and the job in question; have good interpersonal and in particular communication skills; and be comfortable working as a group facilitator. They also stress pitfalls to be avoided by job analysts such as being judgmental, and the tendency to turn job analysis into counselling sessions.

A final issue which ought not to be omitted is that it would be unwise to assume that systematic job analysis provides all the answers. A job analysis of the headteacher's position may identify the skills requirement for the job, but it does not identify the level at which these skills are to be achieved. Jobs are also dynamic entities, they are not static. The job analysis conducted on heads will therefore need at regular intervals to be reviewed, monitored and updated.

Summary and Conclusions

This chapter described job analysis as a systematic process for gathering information about jobs, with the capacity to produce outcomes relevant to schools, and as a form of applied research. There are three major approaches to job analysis – task/ job orientated, behaviour/job holder methods and attribute/trait strategies. A number of practical issues must be considered prior to commencing a job analysis study.

The chapter reviewed some job analysis techniques and presented the advantages and disadvantages associated with each technique. The choice of appropriate method(s) will depend on the aim and desired outcomes to the job analysis investigation, and on concerns of an operational nature.

A number of significant issues underlying the application of a systematic job analysis process to the headteacher position have also been highlighted. For example, whether the analysis should focus on the head's job as it is currently performed or as it should be performed; a value-driven rather than objective approach to analysis aimed at eliciting information on the head's future job role; the influence on job analysis results of time, person, and context factors; and the role of the job analyst.

Note

1 'The Occupational Personality Questionnaire', 'OPQ' and 'SHL' are registered trademarks ® Saville and Holdsworth Ltd.

Chapter 2

Management Competencies

Introduction

The chapter considers the potential benefits to be derived from the application of a competency-based approach to education management. Competencies and competency-based assessment procedures have not to date achieved widespread usage in the education sector. In their appropriate use, robustly generated and validated, competencies present the best vehicle presently available to us for an objective diagnosis of development and training needs, and a systematic approach to selection and recruitment. There are potential benefits in adopting a competence framework for staff working in school at all levels; the focus here however is on the application of a competency-based approach to senior managerial positions in school and in particular to the post of headteacher.

Competency-based assessment in the UK is in the form of two major approaches. The first uses methods emanating from a 'personal qualities' approach to competence deriving from research conducted in the early 1980s by Richard Boyatzis and McBer and Company (although the origination of such approaches is earlier than this). The second uses techniques of competency-based assessment adopting an occupational standards approach as promoted by the present government to detail the standards required for all work roles.

The topic of competence and competency-based assessment seems to be bedeviled in educational circles with misconception and misunderstanding. This chapter therefore aims to resolve and clarify issues surrounding competencies, particularly where there is currently confusion, by examining competencies at the levels of conceptualization; competency derivation; and competence assessment.

The chapter is divided into three sections. The first section, 'A framework for conceptualizing competence', examines the two apparently disparate approaches to the generation and use of competencies and attempts to draw together the two approaches into a unifying conceptual framework. It also presents some of the major criticisms levelled at competence approaches and argues for competencies to be viewed at the very least as the basic building blocks in describing a headteacher's job performance.

Section 2 on 'selecting a suitable approach to competence', while regarding the two approaches to competence as complementary, discusses some factors guiding the choice of a methodology which is appropriate to purpose. Differences between the two approaches as to how competencies are derived are also presented. A case for the adoption of an approach embracing 'generic' competencies is examined and the relationship of the latter to competencies which are specific to the occupation, the organization, and the individual, are outlined.

Section 3 centres on 'measuring and assessing an individual's competence' beginning with a brief focus on selected means of assessing competence currently in use. This is followed by a consideration of some underlying issues in assessing competence such as its relationship with performance; the place of knowledge and understanding; and the influence of time. The chapter ends with a discussion summarizing some of the major conclusions.

Before examining competencies at a detailed level, however, there is a need to consider the advantages to schools and to education management of adopting a competency-based approach.

What Can a Competency-Based Approach Offer to Education Management?

A competency-based approach may provide a comprehensive and accurate picture of an education manager's job, and contribute to a better understanding of those factors associated with effective leadership. Such a structured description may even go some way towards theory building in education management, and provide a nationally recognized framework for appraising an education manager's current performance. The latter could lead to standardized procedures which are both systematic in approach and consistent across use by different individuals for recruitment and selection; for promotion; for training; and for assessment leading to personal and/or career development.

Derek Esp (1993) in *Competencies for School Managers* describes 30 or more practical ways to use a competency framework. These include: individual development, appraisal, whole school review, team development, and staff selection and recruitment. We might also add the identification of skill banks and deficiency areas, and the identification of areas of job match and mismatch, in facilitating more effective school development and planning. A more detailed discussion of assessing and developing individuals using competency-based approaches is provided in Chapter 5.

Competencies are a valuable source for reflection upon one's own performance. Evidence suggests that job holders find competencies useful for identifying individual strengths and weaknesses (Schroder 1989; Lyons and Jirasinghe 1992). The *process* of reflection and self-evaluation seems as valuable as the outcome to the assessment.

Employment law and the legal obligations placed upon heads and governors with regard to equal opportunities and fair and non-discriminatory selection practice have already been mentioned in Chapter 1. It represents another decisive argument for the application of competence approaches to schools. Any selection and recruitment procedure which alleviates bias and subjectivity and consequently raises the objectivity of assessment, and which is also seen to be fair, valid and cost effective (Jirasinghe and Lyons 1995), ought to be welcomed by the field of education management.

The discussion has highlighted a number of advantages for embracing an approach which is competency-based in the schools sector. In applying a competency model to education management, however, we need clear information about differential approaches to competence usage presently available, their respective advantages and disadvantages, and the most appropriate strategy for our particular purposes in education management. The next sections of the chapter therefore aim to examine these issues.

Section 1: A Framework for Conceptualizing Competence

The section begins with a brief review of the history and background to competency-based assessment. The two major approaches to competence – the McBer approach and the occupational standards approach – are described. The 'language of competence' is examined and a framework is developed for conceptualizing competencies, for example where each competency is viewed as a 'spectrum'. The major criticisms of the competence approach are discussed, and it is advocated that competencies form the basic building blocks to assessing individuals.

Background and History

Knott (1975) states that amongst the earliest references to competence are those of John Dewey, in *Experience and Education*, and W.W. Charters in the *Commonwealth Study* of 1929 who formalized a proposal for a competence-based teacher education curriculum.

Competence-based assessment has been popular in American industrial/occupational psychology since the late 1960s and early 1970s (Hooghiemstra 1992). It emerged in response to the need to find a form of assessment capable of predicting job performance but which did not discriminate against groups of people. David McClelland is usually credited in this field as the originator of the competency-based approach to assessment (McClelland 1973).

Competency led approaches to the work of school leaders in the USA were also ongoing in the 1970s. Notable in this work were the publications of Lloyd McCleary of the University of Utah, who was also editing the *Competency Notebook*. It was also in the 1970s as a National Board of Education backed approach, that the National Association of Secondary School Principals (NASSP) were generating competencies for high school principals to underpin their Assessment Centre.

The approach which was later to have significant impact upon the practice of management in the UK, however, was that propounded by Richard Boyatzis, usually referred to in the UK as the McBer approach.

The Two Approaches to Competence

There are two major approaches to competence currently in use in the UK: the McBer approach and the occupational standards approach.

1. The McBer approach

In the late 1970s the American Management Association (AMA) commissioned a US consultancy, the McBer Corporation, to conduct a major research exercise to determine those characteristics of managers which distinguished 'superior' performers from only 'average' performers. This work was reported by Richard Boyatzis (Boyatzis 1982).

The McBer approach postulates that effective action or performance will only occur when three critical components concerning the job are consistent or 'fit' together. These are:

- the job's requirements or demands on the individual;
- the characteristics or abilities which enable an individual to demonstrate appropriate actions, called competencies, and representing the capability an individual brings to the job;
- the context of an organization, encompassing internal factors such as organizational policies, procedures, mission, culture, resources etc., and external factors such as the social, political, and economic environment.

The interaction between these elements is shown in Figure 2.1.

Figure 2.1: A model of effective job performance

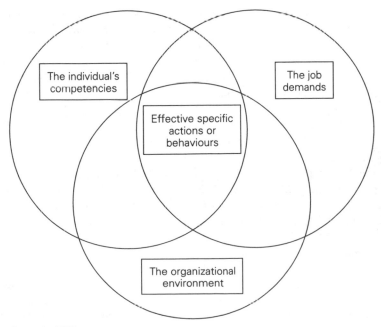

Source: Boyatzis 1982

Boyatzis uses a definition of a competency as: 'an underlying characteristic of a person which results in effective and/or superior performance in a job' (Klemp 1980). He goes on to describe several important features of a competency:

- A competency can be a motive, trait, skill, aspect of one's self-image or social role, or a body of knowledge which he or she uses.
- Each competency may exist within the individual at various levels, with motives and traits at the unconscious level, and skills at the behavioural level.
- A competency is context dependent, that is, given a different organizational environment, the competency may be evident through other specific actions.

The McBer competencies are presented in Appendix 5.

2. The occupational standards approach

The occupational standards approach to competence differs from the McBer approach in that it describes the outcomes that a manager or management team has to achieve in order to demonstrate competent performance. The standards, while accepting that qualities, skills, and knowledge are important, pronounce that the primal task must be to determine the details of competent performance for any particular work role. The standards attempt to provide benchmarks or specifications against which management performance can be assessed. This approach has defined competence very broadly as: 'the ability to perform the activities within an occupation or function to the standards expected in employment' (Training Agency 1988).

The occupational standards approach has been adopted by the government through the Employment Department's Training Enterprise and Education Department (TEED), to detail the standards required for all work roles in the UK. This has led to the creation of occupational sector-specific 'lead bodies' representing employer, employee, and educational interests, the lead body for management being the National Forum for Management Education and Development (NFMED) with its operating arm the Management Charter Initiative (MCI). The standards also form the basis for a national system of accreditation through National Vocational Qualifications (NVQs) administered through the National Council for Vocational Qualifications (NCVQ).

The standards divide work into progressively smaller constituent parts (see Figure 2.2). A 'key purpose' for the job is outlined at the outset with subdivisions according to 'key roles'. 'Units' then describe key task areas, whereas 'elements' are more precise descriptions of what individuals should be able to do. For each element there are associated 'performance criteria' which define characteristics of competent performance of the elements. Additionally, for each element there is a

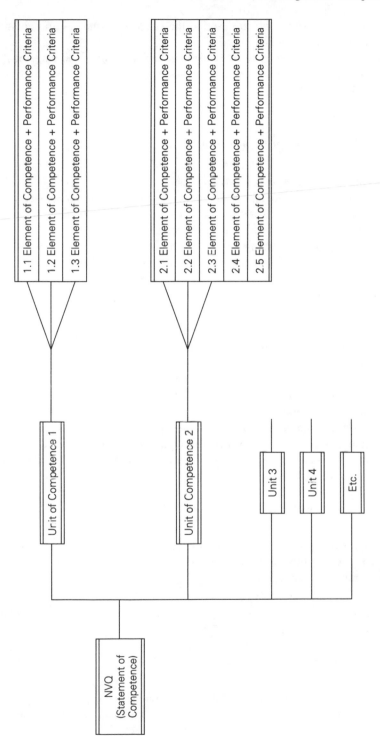

Figure 2.2: The framework for National Vocational Qualifications

Source: Training Agency 1988

set of 'range statements' which describe the range of instances and situations in which the element is applied.

An Employment Department funded project, the School Management South Project, has used this framework to devise specific standards for school management (see Earley 1992).

The Language of Competence

Before considering how these two approaches to competence might be brought together and made to fit into an overarching rationale of competence rather than existing as separate methodologies, it is appropriate to provide some definitions of terms commonly used when describing competencies.

In seeking simple working definitions there is a need to look at what is meant by the terminology surrounding competence. Some commonly occurring terms and their definitions are presented below although it should be emphasized that these are in no way offered as exhaustive definitions.

- *behaviour*: a generic term covering acts, activities, responses, operations, etc., in short, any measurable response of an individual;
- *knowledge*: the body of information possessed by a person;
- *skill*: the capacity for carrying out complex, well-organized patterns of behaviour so as to achieve some end or goal;
- *motive*: a characterization of the cause of an individual behaviour;
- *trait*: any enduring characteristic of a person that can serve an explanatory role in accounting for the observed regularities and consistencies in behaviour. It does not constitute the regularities themselves. A trait is a hypothesized, underlying component of an individual's behaviour;
- *ability*: the qualities, talents etc. that enable one to perform a particular feat at a specified time. (from Reber 1985)

A number of assumptions about motives, traits, and abilities and definitions of competence which rely on these elements are indicated by the preceding points. Motives, traits, and abilities:

- play a causal, explanatory role in accounting for the more observable behavioural aspects;
- are all theoretical entities or hypothesized underlying components; which
- may be more difficult to directly measure.

Definitions of competence which rely on behaviours (measurable responses) and knowledge (body of information possessed by a person) or skills (capacity for carrying out patterns of behaviour) do not exhibit the same features. They will therefore tend to be more amenable to direct assessment or measurement.

The Iceberg Model

A practical attempt at drawing together the two competence approaches is to picture the competencies of any one individual as akin to an iceberg (see Figure 2.3). Generally speaking, MCI and NCVQ approaches discussed earlier have tended to concentrate on those features above the water line – the skills and knowledge components – while the McBer approach has emphasized those aspects of managerial behaviour which would be below the water line – the underlying traits/motives etc.

Figure 2.3:   The iceberg model

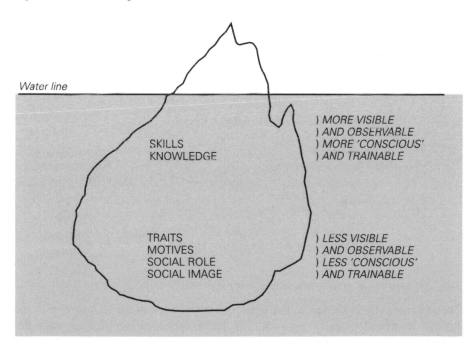

Source: Spencer and Spencer 1993

The definitions provided above have shown that the knowledge and skills possessed by an individual are more visible and observable than his or her traits/motives/social role/social image. The latter are consequently depicted below the water line. It is hypothesized that those qualities below the water line – the traits/motives etc. – enable or give rise to the skilled behaviour above the water line. The skills and knowledge components may also be more responsive to training, while traits and motives may be less likely to alter as a result of training.

An Overview of Competence

Two approaches to competence have been identified: the McBer perspective adopting what is often termed a 'personal qualities' approach to competence definition and the occupational standards approach focusing on performance outcomes. While many would tend to see the tenets of each approach as mutually exclusive it is in fact more appropriate to conceptualize each as emanating from opposite poles of an overarching competency framework where there is much overlap between the constituent parts. This requires some careful explanation.

Job analysis: The same starting point

Both the McBer/personal qualities and occupational standards approaches start from the same point: the identification of job tasks through job analysis. This is illustrated in Figure 2.4. The essential difference is that in the McBer approach the identification of tasks/skills is seen as an intermediate step in the identification of the personal qualities.

Figure 2.4:   Job analysis: The same starting point

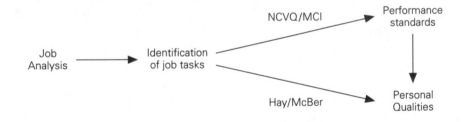

Two different ways of describing the job performed

The starting point is the same, but there is a divergence in the description of the job that is offered by each approach. The McBer/personal qualities approach describes those components of the person that enable him or her to be competent, while the occupational standards approach describes those functions of the job at which the person must be competent. The distinction is essentially between what people need to do in a job with what they need in order to do it effectively.

In returning to the iceberg model depicted in Figure 2.3 then, those aspects of the person that give rise to competent behaviour would be those facets represented below the water line – the traits/motives and so on. The constituents above the water line – the skills and knowledge components – would tend to be job functions.

Competencies can therefore be conceptualized as either:

- behaviours that are traits, motives, or *personal qualities* (e.g. sensitivity, breadth of awareness, reasoning etc.) which enable an individual to be competent, or as,
- behaviours that are more skills-based such as outputs, deliverables, or *standards* (e.g. staff management, customer service etc.), of which the job consists and at which a person may be competent.

The difference between 'competence' and 'competency'

Further confusion surrounds the distinction between the sometimes synonymously used terms 'competency' and 'competence'. Medley *et al.* (1989) have stated that 'competency' is used to refer to any characteristic that enhances a job holder's ability to perform effectively. 'Competence' however, is used to refer to the possession of a specified set of competencies. In other words: Competence = Competency 1 + Competency 2 + Competency 3 and so on, where Competency 1 can be an occupational standard, an ability/trait, etc.

To summarize then, an individual's 'competence' can be thought of as the degree to which he or she has been found to exhibit the 'competencies' which have been derived through job analysis as being important for effective job performance. These competencies may be conceptualized as either a part of the *person* performing the job, as represented by traits, motives, and personal qualities, or as part of the *job* being performed, as depicted by skills-based outputs and occupational standards. Both fit into an overarching framework of competence, the difference arising as a variation in the 'description' of competence offered. This description may be at the level of the person carrying out the job, and the attributes necessary for effective performance, or at the level of the job being performed, and the job areas/functions which must be effectively performed.

A Competency as a Spectrum

A framework has been developed summarizing some of the major elements in conceptualizing competencies (see Figure 2.5). The competencies shown along the x axis (C1, C2, C3 etc.) are each represented as consisting of both skills components, and traits, motives, and personal qualities. Observability is shown along the y axis, the skills components of the competencies being more visible and easily observable than traits and motives. Knowledge components are additionally depicted alongside the skills since they are also more observable than traits, motives and personal qualities.

Traits, motives and personal qualities are shown as fitting into the McBer approach to competence while the skills and knowledge components project onto the NCVQ/MCI perspective on competence. The framework in Figure 2.5, while useful and accurate at a generalized level, nevertheless represents a rather polarized version of the situation. For example the wide definition of a competency adopted by the McBer approach acknowledges skill and knowledge components as well as

Figure 2.5:   *A framework for conceptualizing competencies*

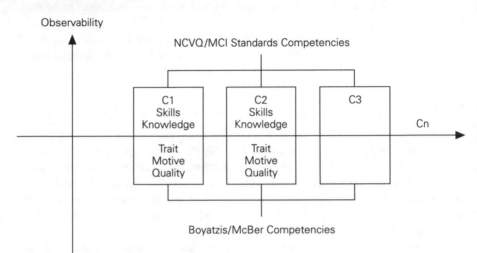

the trait and motive elements. It is difficult also when examining competency lists which currently exist, to designate a set of competencies as representing either skills or personal qualities. The majority of current lists appear to be a hotchpotch of both.

It is suggested that each competency is best pictured as a spectrum of colour running from red to violet, where the red light corresponds to underlying traits/ motives and the violet light accords to skills/knowledge. The colours in between represent areas of overlap of skill and trait definitions (see Figure 2.6).

Figure 2.6:   *A competency as a spectrum*

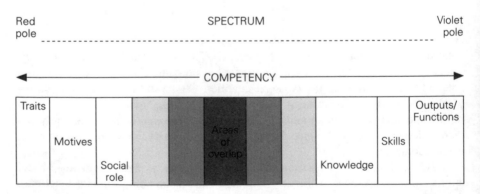

The McBer approach would seem mainly to draw a picture of competence utilizing the red trait/motive extremity of the spectrum; the occupational standards approach tends toward the violet skills end of the spectrum. Competence models however may draw up a given competency at any point along this spectrum. The composition of the competencies, in quota terms of traits, skills and so on will therefore vary across different competence models. One model may be characterized by competencies which are equally skills and trait-based, while another may consist of competencies in a ratio of 80 per cent traits and 20 per cent skills/performance outcomes.

Criticisms of the Competence Approach

So far the authors have offered an overview of competence and a framework for conceptualizing competencies without criticism. There are some theorists and practitioners however who have objections to the concepts underlying competencies and their assessment at a fundamental level:

- Do competencies as a construct exist at all? Competencies, it is claimed, are of unclear logical status (Ashworth and Saxton 1990). Are they mental or physical characteristics of a person? Are they pieces of behaviour or is it the outcome of behaviour?
- An assessment of competence does not reflect the cognitive processes underlying performance. Individuals all achieving the same competency standard may do so by utilizing a variety of disparate cognitive operations.
- Successful results may be accomplished through the application of many strategies. The example of the school head who prefers to work with facts rather than figures and consequently delegates day to day fiscal management to a proficient deputy/bursar provides a case in point. Deliberative steps are taken by the head to offset personal disinclination and the outcome is one of effective financial management. Can the head in this example be deemed to have displayed a 'competent' performance although results have not been achieved through direct personal performance?
- Competency approaches reduce jobs into lists of highly circumscribed task elements, skills, or personal characteristics.
- Management is a highly complex interactive process. It does not fit easily with the competency approach's additive methodology of summing long lists of competencies to produce 'global' competence. Elements of skill or ability are interdependent and interrelated and not separable from the complex whole. Attainment of one competency cannot be divorced from the attainment of another (related) competency.
- Competency-based approaches do not truly reflect the subtleties of the individual context or social environment in which jobs are performed. An appreciation of the latter is essential for an understanding of behaviour constituting effective job performance.
- The competence movement underemphasizes the competencies that go with innovation and fosters a regulative view of managing (Vaill 1983). Competency approaches are accused of maintaining the status quo and of failing

to prescribe the competencies necessary to operate in new and dynamic environments.

- Competency-based assessment techniques neglect some qualities/abilities, such as creativity, which are not amenable to direct observation and measurement but which are nevertheless crucial for effective job performance (Jacobs 1989).
- The flatter management structures and flexible working patterns now increasingly advocated predicate a shift from analyzing competencies for individuals to analyzing competencies for teams of people working together. Belbin (1981) has argued for a team constructed with a balance of talents and strengths, rather than a group of individuals all trained/developed to the same standard.
- The assumption that if we identify the competencies possessed by effective managers, and then teach them to 'learners', the latter will become effective managers, is a logical fallacy (Vaill 1983). By extrapolating this premise to schools we cannot conclude that by training heads to be proficient in those competencies hypothesized to be required for effective performance, or that have been shown by effective heads in the past, that we will attain increased school effectiveness.

Competencies are the Basic Building Blocks

Most opponents to competency-based assessment propose a return to a more 'whole-person' orientated approach to assessing and developing individuals, by the inter-relation of task and skill components, behaviours, knowledge constituents, trait and motive elements, attitudes and social context factors, to arrive at a more holistic understanding of an individual's job performance.

There is much merit in this approach. It would be wrong to conclude from this proposition however that competencies do not also have a part to play. Woodruffe (1992) has asserted that while there *is* more to being a good manager than a set of competencies, the latter form a large part of the recipe. In accepting the head's job as complex and multifarious in nature and consisting of *more* than a list of disjunctive competencies, it does not necessarily follow from this that competencies have no useful purpose. Competencies can provide the basic structure upon which to build 'whole-person' views of an individual. A concentration on the whole-person can only proceed when the basic skills, as represented by competencies, have been mastered. Basic competencies may be generic in nature, applicable across a range of jobs, and will be supplemented by competencies which are more specific to the occupation, the organization, and the individual. True managerial effectiveness will emerge from an integration of all of these elements.

Competencies also have an important advantage over holistic approaches. A practically useful description of the head's job must have the capability to underpin selection and recruitment, management development, training and appraisal processes for heads. It is also vital that these processes address ensuing issues of standardization, objectivity, and equity. Such factors would seem to raise problems for a holistic approach; for example, at the practical level of providing systematic and standardized diagnosis and development.

Section 2: Selecting a Suitable Approach to Competence

This section begins with a consideration of the essential differences between the McBer and the occupational standards methodologies in how competencies are derived/generated. It also highlights a number of factors guiding the selection of an appropriate competency-based approach, and includes an examination of models of competence which aim at being 'generic', and the relationship of these generic competencies to those competencies unique to a particular occupation, organization, and individual.

Deriving Competencies

Competencies are generated by studying the job through a process of job analysis (see Chapter 1). The two approaches to competence described – the McBer and occupational standards approaches – both emanate from this starting point. There are however differences between the two as to the conduct of the job analysis and its utilization in deriving competencies.

The job competence assessment method

McBer and company have developed 'the job competence assessment method' to derive competencies. Boyatzis (1982) used this methodology and information gathered from 2000+ managers in 41 different management jobs in 12 organizations, to uncover 19 management competencies (these are presented in Appendix 5). The method uses a five-step procedure to produce a validated competency model for a job (Klemp 1979). The procedure involves the conduct of 'behavioural event interviews' (similar to critical incident interviews – see Chapter 1) with job holders and others to identify the competencies. The technique compares a group of clearly superior job performers to a sample of average or poor performers, and produces a set of validated characteristics or competencies that have been shown to relate to effective and superior job performance (see Boyatzis 1982, for a fuller explanation).

From the authors' experience it may not however always be appropriate to identify 'superior' from ' average' performers. One might also question the need to refer to superior performers at all; competencies can be based on average performance, or pitched at somewhere in between average and superior performance.

The job competence model has the advantage over other methods in that it is validated in terms of on-the-job performance. Often the competencies resulting from other competency-generation procedures are assumed to be related to performance but are not empirically tested against performance data. There are however good reasons as to why this might occur. Even if it were possible to agree upon a set of performance criteria, theorists such as Sashkin (1991) have been scathing of traditional measures of performance, for example, superordinate ratings. The latter have often been found to be biased, and tend to foster senior members of staff's own 'implicit' theories of leadership and performance, which may in practice have little to do with real performance. For example, a male dominated managerial hierarchy may have an in-built tendency to reinforce the status quo and produce a potential bias against women.

Functional analysis

The occupational standards approach to competence has adopted an alternative methodology to derive competencies – that of functional analysis. Usually conducted in workshop and brainstorming sessions with members of an occupational group, functional analysis is the process of identifying those functions which lead to an organization satisfying its mission or purpose. The process identifies these functions and breaks them down into 'units' and 'elements', until the job functions are described in sufficient detail to be used as occupational standards (see Figure 2.2; and refer to Training Agency Guidance Notes 1988, 1989, Management Charter Initiative 1990, or Earley 1993 for further information). Once completed the results of the analysis are checked with a wider audience, probably through a questionnaire survey of practitioners. Functional analysis has been used by the government in the UK to develop occupational standards for the British workforce.

Functional analysis methods which are based on brainstorming sessions of a small number of middle or senior managers could be criticized on the grounds that they do not canvass the views of a sufficiently large sample of job incumbents to guarantee representativeness. Additionally, the prescription of occupational standards by superiors introduces questions of bias, and the maintenance of the status quo. By focusing on what an individual or group of experts think is of relevance, functional analysis could produce an 'espoused theory of action' and not a 'theory in use' (Argyris and Schon 1978).

In deriving a set of competencies both the job competence assessment and functional analysis methodologies described above rely at some stage upon reaching a consensus as to the most appropriate 'clustering' of information collected through the job analysis. There might potentially be an infinite number of combinations of tasks, skills and abilities to form a cluster of associated tasks, skills etc., or competencies. The process is however likely to be influenced by several factors: issues of particular concern to the schools sector, the context factors relating to the job under study, and issues of a historical/custom/political nature.

Only two methods of competency derivation have been described here, but others are also available (see Boam and Sparrow 1992 for a review of these). Whatever methods are used, the more sophisticated and thorough the job analysis conducted, the more accurate and relevant the competencies identified are likely to be.

The Personal Qualities and Standards Approaches Compared:
Some Factors Guiding the Selection of a Particular Approach

In Chapter 1 it was asserted that the choice of an appropriate job analysis technique should be led by the purpose of the investigation, the specific job under study, and issues of an operational nature. Similarly the choice of an approach based on the McBer model or the occupational standards model will depend upon the aim and function of the derived set of competencies. For example:

- Are the competencies for selection and recruitment, management development, or appraisal?
- Is it current or future performance that is the primary interest?
- Is assessment to be work-based or carried out elsewhere?

Also the particular job under study must be of concern. For example:

- What is the level of the position – clerical, technical, supervisory, managerial?
- Is performance data available or obtainable – is it possible to compare 'superior' with 'average' performers? Are there political/custom/cultural issues to consider?
- How will the competence model adopted be received by the occupational sector or organization?

A third consideration is are there limiting factors in operational terms? For example,

- What resources are available to develop and apply the competence model?

In the sections which follow attention is focused on five important areas in the choice of an appropriate competence model/approach:

- values and ethical issues;
- job context;
- the tendency towards a 'list culture';
- assessing future management potential; and the
- occupational level/grade.

Values and ethical issues

The McBer approach or an equivalent which is based on 'personal qualities' has scope and flexibility for the incorporation of values, philosophy and beliefs guiding and underpinning an individual's actions. Traditionally one of the major objections to a totally standards-based approach has been the claim that it neglects these 'ethical' aspects of job performance. In the past few years however considerable progress has been made to include ethical criteria and value statements in developing occupational standards. A report sponsored by the Employment Department and carried out by the Management and Professional Development Unit of the University of Sussex (Employment Department Learning Methods Branch 1994) has expressed the view that the incorporation of ethical issues is crucial to the effectiveness and credibility of occupational standards.

Unfortunately many standards in place at present do not seem to allow sufficiently for the ethical issues underlying an individual's work performance. For example the standards developed by the MCI for managers across all occupational sectors at NVQ levels 3, 4 and 5, while laden with terms which *imply* value judgments, make no attempt to develop the ethical dimensions which underlie the standards (Employment Department Learning Methods Branch 1994). Recommendations of ethical codes of practice to accompany occupational standards may be insufficient to ensure the prominence of values in competency assessment but need to be explicitly incorporated into the definitions of competencies.

Job context

One of the major criticisms mentioned earlier by those opposing competency-based assessment is the perceived tendency by the competence approach to isolate competence from job context. In practice both the McBer and the occupational standards approaches try to accommodate job context in their assessment of an individual's competence, but in different ways. The McBer approach highlights the importance of job context by stating that competent performance will only occur when an individual's competencies correspond to job demands and the organizational environment, that is the internal and external factors impinging upon an organization (see Figure 2.1).

The occupational standards approach advocates the use of 'range statements', describing 'the range of contexts and applications in which a competent person would be expected to achieve the outcome or Elements' (Training and Development Lead Body 1992). A specification of the range of contexts in which competence is to be demonstrated is not however a substitute for an assessment of competence which reflects the influence of the organizational climate/environment on an individual's actions/behaviour. Where the latter is seen as a necessary and essential part of an individual's competence assessment the occupational standards approach may not, at least in its entirety, be sufficient.

The tendency towards a 'list culture'

One criticism which is often levelled at the occupational standards approach is its tendency to produce long 'lists of performance criteria', which prove bureaucratic (Everard 1990) and are too detailed to be practicable. For example, Earley (1993) working with school management standards, has reported that the costs of working with the standards – both in terms of time and money – was a commonly voiced concern amongst those using the standards in schools. It should be stated however that the production of long lists of performance criteria is a practice which is discouraged by the NCVQ and in Lead Body guidance, particularly at higher NVQ levels.

Potential benefits from the generation of such lists of performance criteria arise where there is a need for a specific and very detailed elucidation of tasks constituting job performance, rather than a more restricted and 'abstracted' set of competencies.

Assessing future management potential

Competencies adopting a McBer or occupational standards framework, which are based on current performance or past practice, may become out-of-date very quickly. Thus any competence model which is not sufficiently future-orientated may not be an indicator of future management potential.

The occupational level/grade

In the case of senior managerial jobs, multiplicity of tasks and roles and the level of complexity diminish the likelihood of adequately describing these positions by means of a list of tasks or performance indicators. It is sometimes suggested that the standards approach may be more suited to lower level, non-management type jobs, while the multiple and complex roles taken on by managers may mean that the standards must be supplemented (if not replaced) by a more personal 'qualities' approach (Ouston 1991; Jirasinghe and Lyons 1995).

The standards approach does acknowledge the importance of those personal characteristics guiding effective performance, particularly in relation to senior managers. For example, the MCI standards have a set of 'personal competencies' (also referred to as the 'personal effectiveness model') to be used alongside their occupational standards for managers, although greater clarity is required as to how the former are to be integrated with the latter in making an inference of competence.

The Two Approaches to Competence: An Antithetical or Symbiotic Relationship?

Some theorists would regard each of the two main approaches to competence as mutually exclusive and essentially antithetical. It was proposed earlier by the authors that each approach should be conceptualized as issuing from opposite ends of an overarching competency continuum or spectrum. The descriptions of the job produced by the two approaches – 'person-orientated' for McBer and 'output/ function orientated' for the occupational standards – are both equally valid, and no singular approach is perpetually expedient.

The issue should not be one of a competition with one approach appearing as victor, but of a complementary and symbiotic relationship where each approach has recognized strengths and weaknesses predicating adoption according to circumstance and appropriateness to purpose.

The Case for Generic Competencies

In certain circumstances the most suitable model of competence may be one which aims to be 'generic', that is, it presents the skills or personal qualities shown by individuals in the same job/position across a range of organizations. A generic skill is also seen as transferable between different occupations. This is the definition adopted in the UK and in the context of this book. It is worth mentioning here however that the term 'generic' differs in meaning in the USA, where it is used to denote the 'encompassing of a wide variety or whole class of behaviours' (CNAA/ BTEC 1990).

One of the key parts of the UK government's standards development programme is the undertaking by the NFMED/MCI to produce competencies that are required of 'most managers all of the time', i.e. competencies that are generic to management, whatever the area of employment. It is intended that this will provide a unifying framework for management development courses and their assessment and accreditation. The NFMED/MCI model for, for example middle managers (Management II), has 36 elements and 10 units. Each of the elements of competence, in turn, has between 4 to 10 performance criteria. In adopting a generic framework however, a personal qualities approach may be more generally applicable to managers working in different contexts than an approach such as the MCI focusing on specific job tasks and functions.

There is a strong case to be made for the use of generic headteacher competencies. Headteachers with demonstrable competence in school management should be able to work in a variety of comparable organizational or occupational settings. Resultant opportunities for exchange of information across diverse organizational contexts and professional domains, for personal development and career progression seem attractive. A nationally recognized set of generic headteacher competencies could also be used to form the basis for a system of selection and recruitment, management development, appraisal and training, which is collective and standardized.

The major advantage associated with the exercise of generic competencies – their generality – also belies the major objection to their use, that of ignoring the specific demands of a particular job. It is axiomatic that the generic methodology neglects the influence of specific context, social, cultural, and political factors affecting performance.

The McBer approach to competence does go some way in alleviating this criticism; for example a consideration of the internal and external organizational environment is seen as crucial to the assessment of effective performance. The McBer model provides a picture of what competencies one would *expect to find* in effective managers regardless of the individual situational context, but does not specify that a manager with such competencies will be effective in a particular job in a specific organization.

It is probable that there are many common elements in a list of competencies equally germane to similar jobs in separate organizations; the problem is that typically generic lists are seen as applicable in their entirety. It is preferable however if the specification of a set of generic competencies does not imply its application absolutely. The set of generic competencies should be used as a reference point, with shifts in emphasis, reprioritizations, or indeed additions, to the specified competencies according to salient contextual influences.

Job Competencies: Generic, Occupational, Organizational and Individual

A headteacher's job may be conceived as composed of generic or core elements held in common with other (similar) jobs. Dulewicz (1989) postulated that generic constituents would account for about 70 per cent of the competencies necessary for effective performance. There would also appear to be tasks, and at a more abstracted level competencies, which are of critical importance to the education sector particularly, and where points of difference would emerge when comparison is made with other occupational sectors.

We would also suggest a third level of competency, comprising competencies specific first at an 'organizational' level, and second, at an 'individual' level. Some competencies may be the result of issues which are context driven – these might for example relate to school size, school sector/phase, or be a salient feature of an inner-city school with high levels of social deprivation. Other competencies may be a consequence of individual headteacher preference, personal style, idiosyncrasy, a distinctive school history and so forth. The relationship between these various job competencies is summarized in Figure 2.7.

Figure 2.7:   The relationship between different job competencies

Generic management competencies

Occupational sector specific competencies

Individual and/or organizational specific competencies

Recognizing that both organizational and individual context factors have a part to play, it is likely that there are a greater number of underlying similarities in the ways that schools are managed than dissimilarities. Thus variations of an organizational or individual nature may only produce differences in emphasis, prioritization or urgency, to a specified set of generic competencies for headteachers, rather than altering the set of competencies *per se*.

Section 3: Measuring and Assessing an Individual's Competence

The earlier sections of this chapter have considered competencies at a number of important levels, for example those of conceptualization and derivation. The one area not yet discussed remains that of how competencies are measured and assessed in order to arrive at an inference of competence. This section will therefore focus on matters surrounding the assessment of competence, for example, some techniques utilized in appraising competence. Additionally underlying issues such as the relationship between 'competence' and 'performance'; the place of knowledge and understanding in assessing competence; and the influence of time, will also be considered.

Competence Assessment Methods

A brief focus is presented here on four selected means of assessing competence: self-evaluation, portfolios, psychometric testing, and assessment centres. The discussion is in no way intended to be an exhaustive review of techniques employed in assessing the competence of headteachers. There are many other forms of assessment currently in use, including interviews, references and biodata, presentations, and of course the appraisal process. The purpose here is not to debate the merits of each of these methodologies; this has been succinctly accomplished elsewhere (see for example, Morgan *et al.* 1984). Rather it is to present the reader with forms of assessment commonly utilized in the context of competency-based assessment, and in other non-educational occupational sectors, which may be applied to the schools sector. The competence assessment procedures presented here have therefore been chosen as illustrative of this purpose.

Self-evaluation

Self-evaluation is of course not new to the education sector; much development and training offered to those who work in schools has included some form of self-assessment. Self-evaluation is an important aspect underpinning competence-based approaches to assessment issuing from either an occupational standards viewpoint or that of a personal qualities outlook.

There are several arguments promoting the use of self-evaluation to support and complement more formalized forms of diagnosis and assessment. First, counter to being subjected to external imposition the individual is allowed to structure/steer their own performance review. This approach is likely to promote a commitment and responsibility by the individual towards his or her assessment and development. The individual is compelled to consider their own strengths and weaknesses, ensuing training and development needs, and their requirements from the organization. Finally if combined with the perspectives of others – for example superordinates, subordinates, and peers – the outcome can be a rigorous and objective assessment of job performance.

Portfolio of competence

In the occupational standards approach to competence assessment candidates may produce 'evidence' which demonstrates competence through their work. By collecting examples of this evidence the candidate can put together a portfolio demonstrating his or her competence across a range of situations. A number of sources of evidence are acceptable, for example:

- workplace assessment – direct observation of work activities by an assessor to assess standards achievement, and also a candidate's knowledge and understanding;
- questioning techniques – elicit supplementary evidence supporting performance data assessing a candidate's requisite values, principles, knowledge and understanding etc. underpinning performance (from the Training and Development Lead Body 1992).

Psychometric tests

The high predictive validity and economy offered by norm-referenced psychometric tests makes their use in an assessment procedure attractive, although the degree to which they are perceived by candidates as being fair, objective, and 'user-friendly' acts as a limiting factor in their widespread use.

Many types of psychometric tests are in use: for example tests measuring general intelligence, verbal ability, numerical ability, spatial reasoning, diagrammatic reasoning and so on. Smith and Robertson (1992) assert that for most jobs the reliability coefficients of ability tests are high, usually 0.8 or 0.9, validity varies between 0.2 and 0.5, and most tests are fair to women and minority groups.

Other forms of psychometric testing include personality tests, motivation and interest inventories. For more information about psychometric testing consult Bethell-Fox (1989) and Toplis et al. (1991).

Assessment centres

An assessment centre is a process in which individuals have an opportunity to participate in a series of situations which resemble what they might be called upon to do in a real work setting. They are tested by situational or simulation exercises (e.g. in-tray exercises; group exercises; role-plays; presentations, etc.) and multiple trained assessors process information in a fair and impartial manner (Jaffee and Sefcik 1980). The use of multiple assessment techniques ensures a comprehensive coverage of attributes and skills while multiple assessors decrease the chances of subjectivity and partiality.

Assessment is based on a set of clearly defined dimensions or competencies, which have been determined by an analysis of relevant job behaviours (Task Force on Assessment Centre Standards 1980). These competencies tend to fit with a personal qualities/McBer framework of competence.

Assessment centres are used for a variety of purposes, including selection and recruitment and assessment of potential for promotion, diagnosis of strengths and development needs for training and management development, career planning, and so forth. Evidence on equal opportunities and assessment centres also tends to be favourable; the assessment centre method is therefore identified as especially attractive for affirmative action such as the accelerated advancement of minority groups and women.

Studies have indicated a strong positive relationship between assessment centre ratings and job performance. Schmitt *et al.* (1984) have compared validity studies using different types of performance predictors and report the mean predictive validity for assessment centres as 0.407. Gaugler *et al.* (1987) suggest that the validity of assessment centres lies between 0.33 and 0.53 when statistical artefacts have been corrected for. Assessment centres are discussed in greater detail in Chapter 5.

The Relationship between Competence and Performance

In addition to selecting an accurate, reliable and valid means of appraising an individual's competence, other issues surrounding the assessment of competence require resolution. For example, the relationship between competence and performance needs to be clarified. Questions surrounding the relationship between competence and job performance include: what should be acceptable as minimal performance? Should performance measured be optimal or minimal?

Medley *et al.* (1989), working with initial teacher trainees, has been influential in suggesting a distinction between assessing competence and assessing performance.

- *Performance* is the actual behaviour that is exhibited when the individual is working. It refers to what the individual does.
- *Competence* is the individual's capacity to perform. It refers to what the individual is able to do.

Competence, as defined here, is then a prerequisite, but does not guarantee, satisfactory performance. Medley *et al.*'s emphasis for example is on measuring how much knowledge a teacher possesses, and not on how successful he or she is in using it in class. Certain situational factors – e.g. place of employment, range of pupil abilities and attitudes to school – will be beyond a beginning teacher's control and therefore competence certification is based not on performance, but on competence inferred from performance.

Elliott (1989) has also distinguished competence from performance. Competence is a state of being or capacity, and represents underlying and internal powers, while performance is its outward manifestation. Thus individuals may not always fully display their competence in their outward, public behaviour.

There are two important points with regard to the relationship between competence and performance. Competence it would seem must be *inferred* from performance, and the impact of situational and environmental factors fully appreciated in measuring and assessing an individual's competence. Second, although it is necessary in seeking to make an assessment of an individual to strike a balance, it should be recognized that competence may not necessarily lead to effective performance.

The Place of Knowledge and Understanding in Competence Assessment

'Knowledge' is defined as the ownership of facts, theories, principles, etc. required for competent performance. 'Understanding' encompasses the way in which knowledge is organized internally and how it is applied in different contexts (Black and Wolf 1990). Both the occupational standards and the McBer approach acknowledge the significance of knowledge and understanding in attesting to an individual's competence, although differences arise in the incorporation of these elements into competence assessment.

The McBer/personal qualities approach to competence by representing competencies as the 'capabilities an individual brings to the job' has a great deal of flexibility for the inclusion of elements of knowledge and understanding in arriving at an evaluation of competence.

Mansfield (1990) identifies a more fundamental position of the occupational standards approach, that while knowledge and understanding play an essential role in achieving competence, it need not be directly evident in the structure of standards themselves since the latter are to do with performance. Knowledge is used as an additional or alternative source of evidence where performance evidence is exhausted. The knowledge component, it is claimed, is evident in performance and does not therefore have to be considered separately.

Some theorists (Eraut 1990; Wolf 1990) have however been concerned with distinguishing between what Eraut has called 'knowledge displayed in performance' and 'knowledge underpinning performance'. The latter it is argued requires direct assessment of knowledge components. Wolf has disputed that knowledge and understanding elements are inextricably linked to performance. Knowledge and understanding are constructs which have to be inferred from observable behaviour (performance), just as much as competence itself.

Such reasoning has been influential in compelling the occupational standards approach to readdress the issue of knowledge and understanding in competence assessment. To this effect, a report on the place of knowledge and understanding in the development of NVQs has clarified the standards' position on the matter (Employment Department 1994).

A consideration of knowledge and understanding is seen as *essential* in the development of standards and its description a necessary step to specifying the evidence required to make a safe inference for each element of competence. Thus the role of knowledge and understanding is made explicit in developing 'descriptors' supporting the achievement of the standards, and at the practical level of assessment in evidence gathering, although these knowledge components are still not made explicit in the standards themselves.

The 'descriptors' of knowledge and understanding are distinct from the standards, but are justifiable and relevant to the elements, associated performance criteria and range indicators. Knowledge evidence is viewed as complementing performance evidence, each providing a unique perspective.

In contrast to the earlier fundamental position identified by Mansfield (1990), most proponents of an occupational standards-based approach to competence would support the insufficiency of performance evidence alone to measure competence. A separate evaluation of knowledge components complementing performance evidence is recommended.

Job Competencies and the Influence of Time

The exercise of a competency by a head may be continuous, sequential, occur intermittently or as required. Further, while some competencies were essential in gaining entry to the profession, their use may be less pertinent as the head progresses through his or her employment. Thus the influence of time may have an important bearing on competence assessment.

Boam and Sparrow (1992) have viewed competencies as having a lifecycle, such that different competencies will be important at different times during an organization's life. They have categorized four types of competencies each with its own particular 'shelf-life' (see Figure 2.8).

'Emerging' competencies are those that may not be particularly relevant now but will become increasingly important in the future. These competencies are counterbalanced by 'maturing' competencies, which have played an important role in the past but now have a less prominent impact.

'Transitional' competencies come into play during a period of change. These competencies are an integral part of the change process and are required, for example, as a manager embarks upon a new venture. Such competencies may only be relevant for a short period of time at the start of a project, and may be overlooked or replaced when more constant competencies are identified (Boam and Sparrow 1992). Finally there are enduring 'core' competencies; these are continuous and stable and remain as important today as they were previously.

Table 2.1 uses the Boam and Sparrow framework and provides exemplars focusing on the job of headteacher.

It becomes important for individuals to display different competencies at varying stages in an organization's life. However it is not merely the organization which

Figure 2.8: Competency lifecycles

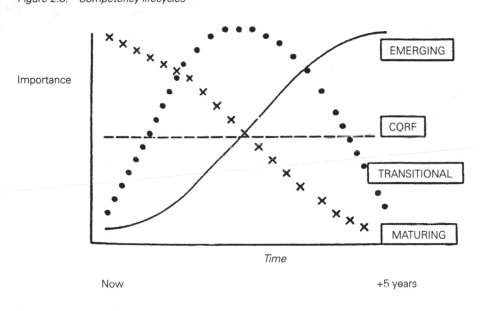

Source: Boam and Sparrow 1992

Table 2.1: Adopting a competency lifecycle framework for headteachers

Headteacher Competencies			
Emerging	Maturing	Transitional	Core
Many competencies in this category, e.g.: • public relations/ marketing skills; • fiscal management; • political skills and the need to build networks/ coalitions, etc.	Dealing directly with pupils, through teaching or personally monitoring pupils' work, may be an example of such a competency. It is interesting to note here however that while the head's tasks, responsibilities and therefore emergent competencies have increased in scope and number, few have declined in importance.	Competencies integral to a period of change, e.g.: • living with uncertainty; • coping with conflict; • managing stress; • flexibility; • being open and responsive, etc.	Many competencies in this category, e.g.: • the need to plan both strategically and in the short term; • the need to work with others; • to reason and exercise good judgment, etc.

passes through periods at which certain competencies are more pertinent than others. Individuals will also experience stages of personal and career development and change which will influence their job performance.

Boyatzis and Kolb (1991, 1992) have proposed three modes of growth and adaptation throughout an individual's career. First, a 'performance mode' where an individual is preoccupied with job success and job mastery, characterized by competencies relating to specific job and organizational demands. Second, a 'learning mode' concerned with the pursuit of novelty and variety, exemplified by competencies pertaining to learning skills, self-image and contingent values. Last, the model includes a 'development mode', focused upon the fulfilment of a human or social purpose or 'calling'. The orientation is self-fulfilment and the key abilities related to this mode are those concerned with motives, values and traits. The modes are essentially sequential but are also recursive, and an individual is predominantly in one mode at a particular point in time.

Both the organization and the individual will, it seems, undergo different stages in their outlook and orientation. Problems and conflicts are likely to arise if the organization's requirements demand a set of competencies to be displayed by an individual which are at odds with the competencies of interest to an individual's prevailing 'growth mode'.

The implications from such theorizing are potentially far-reaching. It demands a shift from simplistic notions of competency-evaluation to a complex 'mapping' of types of competencies, to individual and organizational stages of development, and to effective job performance.

Summary and Conclusions

While accepting and recognizing that the management of educational institutions is a complex process, it would be wrong to conclude that this precludes a competency-based approach to the assessment of individuals in such institutions. Several arguments have been put forward regarding the potential benefits of adopting a competency-based approach in education management and in particular for use with headteachers and with other senior members of staff.

Competencies can provide a picture of the basic skills necessary even if building more holistic descriptions of the head's job performance. A specification of competence is likely to comprise those 'generic' skills and abilities which are common to most managerial activity, but may also include some competencies which distinguish the school sector from other employment areas. They may also include those competencies which are specific to a particular school context, and those that are unique to an individual headteacher.

A number of advantages associated with the adoption of a 'generic' set of competencies for headteachers have been outlined. This set of generic competencies need not be viewed as applicable in its entirety in all situations, but rather as a reference point, with changes in prioritization and emphasis, and exclusions or additions to the set, according to the contextual/environmental circumstances of heads.

Competencies may also alter according to time related variation; both the school and the headteacher will experience different stages of outlook and orientation when certain competencies will be more pertinent than others. The implications of this for the training, development, career management etc. of headteachers may be considerable, involving a complex interaction of types of competencies corresponding to distinct organizational and individual career phases, and successful job performance.

There is much confusion surrounding the status of competencies. The two principal approaches to competence – the McBer personal qualities approach and the occupational standards approach – have been described, including the differential methodologies adopted to derive competencies. While each approach has a corresponding starting point, that of job analysis, there is however a divergence in the description of the job that is offered by each approach. The description may be at the level of the person carrying out the job and the attributes necessary for effective performance, comprising traits, motives or personal qualities, and represented by the McBer approach to competence. Alternatively, the description may be at the level of the job being performed, enacted by job areas or functions, outputs and standards, and embodied by the occupational standards approach to competence.

It is suggested that each competency is best pictured as a spectrum where the red light would correspond to underlying traits/motives and the violet light represents skills. Different approaches to competence may tap a given competency at any point along this spectrum; hence approaches will differ according to the proportions of traits/motives/skills/knowledge components contained within their competency definitions.

Support for an appropriate approach to competency definition, derivation, and assessment should be guided by the purpose and function for which the set of competencies will be used, the issues of importance to the profession and particular job under study, and by operational factors. Neither the occupational standards nor the McBer/personal qualities approaches have universal appeal; each has strengths and weaknesses predicating adoption according to suitability. The two approaches to competence should be regarded as bearing a symbiotic rather than antithetical relationship to one another.

Several factors to be considered in embracing a model of competence for headteachers have been highlighted. To this end, a personal qualities approach to the specification of competence for headteachers would seem to be most appropriate. The multiplicity of tasks and roles comprising the job of head reduces the likelihood of its accurate description by means of closely circumscribed 'lists' of tasks or performance criteria.

A personal qualities approach has greater scope and flexibility for the incorporation of values and ethical issues, and knowledge and understanding components underlying effective headteacher performance, than a standards-based approach which must adhere to a rigid structure of units, elements, performance criteria and range statements. The latter are also seen as insufficient in accounting for the influence of the school context/environment on a head's job performance.

Several points have been made regarding the evaluation of competence. For example, some techniques for measuring and assessing competencies have been described, particularly the use of self-evaluation and the assessment centre technique. As regards assessment, 'competence' must be inferred from 'performance' and it should be recognized that the former may not necessarily lead to effective performance. Knowledge and understanding components will also have to be assessed and inferred from performance just as much as competence itself.

Part II

A Job Analysis of Heads

Part II comprises one chapter, Chapter 3. The chapter is divided into four sections and reports the research findings of a national research project on the headteacher's current job in England and Wales, and discusses issues arising from the analysis.

The research used a national sample of 255 heads from across England and Wales, representing all the main school phases, school types, regions, etc., in addition to the key headteacher variables, e.g. experience of headship, number of headships, etc. We were particularly interested in obtaining a substantial enough number of female heads to enable some analysis of the research returns by gender to take place. The details of the sampling can be found in Appendix 1.

The research adopted an integrated task/behavioural approach to job analysis by using two questionnaires: the Work Profiling System (WPS), focusing on key job task and context elements, and the Occupational Personality Questionnaire (OPQ), providing an orientation to heads' preferred behaviours and ways of working. Additional interviews conducted with heads are reported in Part III of the book.

While the research data and initial summaries in the form of a headteacher job description and person specification (see the third section of Chapter 3) are of considerable interest in themselves, this data is used in the final part of the book, Part III, to identify management competencies for headteachers.

Chapter 3

The Research Findings

Introduction

The chapter presents the findings from the two major questionnaires utilized in the research: the Work Profiling System (WPS) and the Occupational Personality Questionnaire (OPQ), and also includes a description of the instruments used. The chapter is divided into four sections. Section 1 focuses on the Occupational Personality Questionnaire. The use of personality questionnaires in an occupational context, the relevance to headteachers, and the structure and background to the OPQ are discussed. The major findings from the OPQ – the personality attributes which seem to characterize headteachers and distinguish them from other non-educational sector professionals and managers, and variations according to gender of head and school sector – are presented.

Section 2 reports on the Work Profiling System, and includes the structure of the questionnaire and its use, and the data obtained from the WPS analysis. The job tasks selected by heads, time management issues, variations across primary and secondary school sectors, and key job context issues are examined.

Section 3 presents an indicative 'job description' and 'person specification' for the job of headteacher derived from research data and analysis.

Section 4 comprises an exploration of issues arising from the research. For example, difficulties and dilemmas are identified, including caveats to the heads' managerial behaviours; gender issues; and the implications for the training, development and recruitment of heads are discussed.

Section 1: The Occupational Personality Questionnaire (OPQ)

Occupational personality questionnaires are widely used in non-educational employment sectors to inform recruitment and selection, management development, and personal and career counselling. There are two basic elements to the rationale behind their use: that individuals with particular interest and personality profiles will be better suited to certain types of jobs than others in terms of job satisfaction; and that personality factors are related to the adequacy with which an individual performs the job in terms of job success. Both issues are highly contentious and engender active debate amongst academics and practitioners.

The Relevance to Headteachers

It was stated in chapter 1 that the results of many job analysis projects indicate that up to 70 per cent of the attributes which are associated with effective job performance are dimensions of personality rather than ability (Saville and Holdsworth 1990a). Many theorists in education management have offered lists of headteacher characteristics related to effective job performance that would reflect qualities which are essentially personality attributes (see for example Manasse 1985; Pipes 1990; Southworth 1990). Qualities often cited include sensitivity, energy and commitment, social confidence, the ability to be empathetic, persuasiveness, and so on. Little or no empirical research has been conducted into the personality dimensions underpinning the discharge of the head's duties.

The complex issue of headteachers' leadership and management styles has been accorded more attention. Studies have described the effects of situational factors such as school sector, the age and size of the school, the geographical location, the degree of social deprivation etc. (Martinko and Gardner 1983; Manasse 1985) on leadership style. Research has also looked at individual differences between heads according to gender of head (Gray 1987; Ozga 1993; Shakeshaft 1993) and length of time in post (Weindling and Earley 1987; Nias *et al.* 1989) and their influence on the leadership and management styles employed by heads. Thus individual and situational differences may dictate preferences in terms of the leadership and management style adopted by the head and the way he or she fulfils job tasks and interacts with others in school.

Certain personality criteria are important in job success and job satisfaction in a particular occupation. These criteria may vary as a result of situational or individual differences and have considerable implications for headteachers. The consequences of this are potentially far-reaching for an informed understanding of the job of headteacher and how it is currently performed; the different ways that heads may manage schools, for example between men and women and those heads working in secondary and primary contexts; the resultant implications for training and management development; and also for recruitment to headteacher posts.

Using Personality Questionnaires in an Occupational Context

The use of personality questionnaires, of proven reliability and validity, properly used by trained professionals with the provision of feedback, and where possible supplemented with information from other sources, can be extremely effective in an occupational context. Relatively few questionnaires however have been designed specifically for use in an occupational setting. Many were constructed for use in a clinical environment, and are also criticized for being dated and of questionable internal reliability (Saville and Munro 1986; Zuckerman 1989).

The contention that there are considerable differences in the personality traits of job holders in different jobs and that these characteristics are correlated with job achievement has many supporters (Herriot 1989; Furnham 1992; Kline 1992, 1993).

It is not a view however which is universally held and in recent years there has been much altercation and controversy surrounding the use of personality questionnaires to predict job success. Blinkhorn and Johnson's (1990: 672) comment that 'there is precious little evidence that even the best personality tests predict job performance' has received the most media attention. Such allegations have however been rebutted (see Fletcher *et al.* 1991; Jackson and Rothstein 1993). For example Jackson and Rothstein have contended that attacks such as those of Blinkhorn and Johnson are based upon generalizations to the field as a whole from criticism of one or two studies; misconceptions regarding validation research; and characterizations of unprofessional practice as being representative of the discipline. Also, they point out the premature conclusions regarding validity from inadequate surveys of the literature.

The focus here is on the findings from the use of one occupational personality questionnaire with headteachers. The questionnaire, the Occupational Personality Questionnaire, developed by Saville and Holdsworth Ltd. (SHL), has the advantages of being designed strictly for occupational use with underlying strengths of clarity and purpose, and of using nationally-based norms. It is of proven reliability and validity, and is widely used in other non-educational sectors. The application of the questionnaire with heads collects for the first time personality data on headteachers in the form of self-perceptions as to their preferred ways of behaving, their personal style, and their favoured team roles.

The Structure of the Occupational Personality Questionnaire

The OPQ is a structured, standardized, multiple-choice questionnaire with the capacity to obtain information objectively on a broad range of work-relevant personality characteristics. The version of the questionnaire used in the study reported here is the OPQ Concept 5.2. This is the most thoroughly researched of all the questionnaires to date, and has been standardized on a nationally representative sample of 2596 British adults; 1385 male and 1567 female, with four responses gender unspecified. Participants in the standardization were aged from 16 to 65, and included about 400 people from ethnic minority groups.

The questionnaire is normative; respondents rate a series of statements on a scale from 'strongly agree' to 'strongly disagree'. There are 248 questionnaire items in total, producing scores on 31 personality scales or dimensions, eight questionnaire items per personality scale.

The profile of individual personality dimensions obtained is divided into three major areas: relationships with people, thinking style, and feelings and emotions. Each of these areas contains between nine to 11 separate personality scales. Each scale is made up of STEN scores running from 1 (low) to 10 (high).[1] The structure of the personality profile, with brief descriptions for each of the scales, is shown in Table 3.1.

As well as providing scores on individual personality dimensions, the OPQ secures a profile of each headteacher's team types, originating from Belbin's (1981)

Table 3.1: The dimensions of the Occupational Personality Questionnaire*

Relationships with People	Assertive	**Persuasive** – Enjoys selling, changes opinions of others, convincing with arguments, negotiates **Controlling** – Takes charge, directs, manages, organizes, supervises others **Independent** – Has strong views on things, difficult to manage, speaks up, argues, dislikes ties
	Gregarious	**Outgoing** – Fun loving, humorous, sociable, vibrant, talkative, jovial **Affiliative** – Has many friends, enjoys being in groups, likes companionship, shares things with friends **Socially confident** – Puts people at ease, knows what to say, good with words
	Empathy	**Modest** – Reserved about achievements, avoids talking about self, accepts others, avoids trappings of status **Democratic** – Encourages others to contribute, consults, listens and refers to others **Caring** – Considerate to others, helps those in need, sympathetic, tolerant
Thinking Styles	Fields of use	**Practical** – Down-to-earth, likes repairing and mending things, better with the concrete **Data rational** – Good with data, operates on facts, enjoys assessing and measuring **Artistic** – Appreciates culture, shows artistic flair, sensitive to visual arts and music **Behavioural** – Analyzes thoughts and behaviour, psychologically minded, likes to understand people
	Abstract	**Traditional** – Preserves well proven methods, prefers the orthodox, disciplined, conventional **Change oriented** – Enjoys doing new things, seeks variety, prefers novelty to routine, accepts changes **Conceptual** – Theoretical, intellectually curious, enjoys the complex and abstract **Innovative** – Generates ideas, shows ingenuity, thinks up solutions
	Structure	**Forward planning** – Prepares well in advance, enjoys target setting, forecasts trends, plans projects **Detail conscious** – Methodical, keeps things neat and tidy, precise, accurate **Conscientious** – Sticks to deadlines, completes jobs, perseveres with routine, likes fixed schedules
Feelings and Emotions	Anxieties	**Relaxed** – Calm, relaxed, cool under pressure, free from anxiety, can switch off **Worrying** – Worries when things go wrong, keyed-up before important events, anxious to do well
	Controls	**Tough minded** – Difficult to hurt or upset, can brush off insults, unaffected by unfair remarks **Emotional control** – Restrained in showing emotions, keeps feelings back, avoids outbursts **Optimistic** – Cheerful, happy, keeps spirits up despite setbacks **Critical** – Good at probing the facts, sees the disadvantages, challenges assumptions

Table 3.1: (cont.)

Energies	**Active** – Has energy, moves quickly, enjoys physical exercise, doesn't sit still **Competitive** – Plays to win, determined to beat others, poor loser **Achieving** – Ambitious, sets sights high, career centred, results orientated **Decisive** – Quick at conclusions, weighs things up rapidly, may be hasty, takes risks **Social desirability response** – Tends to respond in a socially desirable way

* (6) Saville and Holdsworth Ltd

Table 3.2: Scale definitions of team types

Team Types	
Coordinator	Sets the team goals and defines roles. Coordinates team efforts and leads by eliciting respect.
Shaper	The task leader who brings competitive drive to the team. Makes things happen but may be thought abrasive.
Plant	Imaginative, intelligent and the team's source of original ideas. Concerned with fundamentals.
Monitor–Evaluator	Offers measured, dispassionate critical analysis. Keeps team from pursuing misguided objectives.
Resource investigator	Sales person, diplomat, resource seeker. Good improviser with many external contacts. May be easily diverted from task at hand.
Completer	Worries about problems. Personally checks details. Intolerant of the casual and slapdash. Sees project through.
Team worker	Promotes team harmony. Good listener who builds on the ideas of others. Likeable and unassertive.
Implementer	Turns decisions and strategies into manageable tasks. Brings logical, methodical pursuit of objectives to the team.

Table 3.3: Scale definitions of leadership style

Leadership Styles	
Directive leader	Maintains responsibility for planning and control. Issues instructions in line with own perception of priorities.
Delegative leader	Minimal personal involvement. Believes in delegation of tasks and responsibility.
Participative leader	Favours consensus decision making. Prepared to take time over decisions. Ensures involvement of all relevant individuals.
Consultative leader	Pays genuine attention to opinions/feelings of subordinates but maintains a clear sense of task objectives and makes the final decisions.
Negotiative leader	Makes 'deals' with subordinates. Influences others by identifying their needs and using these as a basis for negotiation.

work on team roles. The questionnaire also produces a profile of the head's 'leadership styles', derived from the work of Bass (1981) on leadership or management style. Based on a 'task' versus 'people' orientation, the latter model highlights a preferred style of managing others. Scale descriptions for team types and leadership styles are presented in Tables 3.2 and 3.3 respectively.

Underlying Assumptions in Using the OPQ

The definition and approach to personality adopted is dependent on the particular theory espoused. There are many different models of personality and it is neither possible nor desirable to describe them here (the reader may however wish to consult Kline 1993, or Furnham 1992 for a review of personality theories of relevance in the occupational context).

The OPQ model of personality contains a number of elements or underlying assumptions about personality:

1   Personality is defined as that which is concerned with a person's typical or preferred ways of behaving, thinking or feeling.
2   People vary in their behaviour, that is, there are demonstrable and measurable individual differences between people.
3   Differences in human behaviour are largely stable and enduring. Variations may occur in an individual's behaviour on a day to day basis, but it is likely that there are behaviour styles and personality characteristics which are core and consistent. These will distinguish particular person(s) in such manner that other individuals will find it difficult to replicate the same characteristics. Thus in the occupational context, some people may find the job more exacting since they lack the requisite personality attributes.
4   The OPQ is 'interactionist' in its approach to the nature–nurture debate. That is, behaviour is viewed as an interaction of constitutional factors (i.e. genetic, physiological, hormonal etc.) and environmental circumstances (i.e. life experiences, family, education, sociocultural aspects etc.). Constitutional factors could account for why those of a similar background behave in different ways (From Saville and Holdsworth 1990a).

The Reliability and Validity of the Questionnaire

Reliability is concerned with the consistency of measurement of the OPQ. The alpha reliabilities of the questionnaire used in this study, the OPQ CM5.2, for the UK general population, range from 0.57 to 0.88 for the 31 scales, with an average of approximately 0.75 (Saville and Holdsworth 1991).

Validity seeks to establish that the OPQ measures what it was designed, or is being used, to measure. The development stages of the OPQ have paid particular regard to the content and face validity of the questionnaire (Saville and Holdsworth

1990a). The issue of criterion validity, that is, the relationship between scores on the OPQ and job performance, has been examined by Robertson and Kinder (1993) using a set of 20 validation studies involving the OPQ and meta-analysis techniques. On average the results showed mean sample size-weighted validity coefficients of the order of 0.20 for the personality variables, with higher values (up to 0.33) for criteria such as creativity and judgment.

Administration, Scoring and Analysis

Standardized procedures were adopted throughout questionnaire administration. Respondents were told that there were no right and wrong answers and that they should answer questions from a work point of view.

The questionnaire was computer-scored by Saville and Holdsworth. Responses were quantified, and compared with a relevant norm group; the norm group most appropriate for our purposes was the managerial/professional group, standardized on 728 respondents.

The outcome was a profile of each head on 31 personality dimensions, and his or her scores on eight team types and five leadership styles. The research sample consisted of 255 headteachers providing usable returns on the OPQ, comprising 113 men (44.3 per cent) and 142 women (55.7 per cent).

A number of statistical analyses were performed on the personality data according to headteacher and school variables. The reporting of findings is focused on the three major areas of:

- headteacher preferences in behaviour, team types and leadership styles, underpinning the discharge of managerial activities;
- variations in preferred behaviours, team types and leadership styles according to gender of head; and
- the influence of school sector/phase on the behaviours, team types and leadership styles favoured by heads.

In presenting the findings we have concentrated on 'patterns' in the data which are consistent. Nevertheless it is wise to be cautious; a project of this magnitude and with such a volume of data may produce spurious results which, although achieving statistical significance, are not meaningful. Although statistical differences between groups of heads are discussed, it is important to bear in mind that individual differences *within* groups, for example within a group of male heads, far outweighs differences found *between* groups, for instance between males and females.

Finally, the questionnaire is a self-report questionnaire and as with all self-report instruments it is prudent to exercise caution in drawing conclusions from data that is based solely on self-perceptions. There may be considerable differences between the latter and the perceptions of others at work with whom the head interacts.

*Analysis of Headteacher Responses to the Occupational Personality
Questionnaire (OPQ): Headteacher Behaviour, Team Role and
Leadership Style Preferences*

While there are a far greater number of individual differences between headteachers,
some commonalities in the choice of behaviours of heads, and in their leadership
styles, were displayed by the heads sampled. These features which seem common
to and are shared by a number of heads may be indicative of those personality
attributes which characterize heads and distinguish them from other professional
domains. The availability of questionnaire norms for non-educational sector profes-
sionals/managers on the Occupational Personality Questionnaire has enabled the
research to make a comparison between headteachers' behaviour preferences and
those of managers in other occupational sectors. The analysis has uncovered the
behaviour, leadership style, and team type preferences which characterize at least
this sample of headteachers.

One of the more remarkable features of the results (refer to Table 3.4) is the
consistent way in which the headteachers' results diverge from those presented for
managers and professionals (those significant at greater than the 1 per cent level are
marked below by an asterisk) although the differences within groups were always
found to be greater than the differences between groups.

For example, in the 'relationships with people' domain heads reported themselves, when compared to the norms for managers and professionals, as more:
persuasive*; controlling*; independent; outgoing; affiliative; socially confident; less
modest, but more democratic* (that is, encouraging others to contribute, consulting
and listening); and more caring. For the 'thinking styles' domain, heads reported
themselves, when compared to the norm for managers and professionals, as more
artistic; more behavioural (that is, likes to understand people, analyzes thoughts and
behaviours); less traditional and more change orientated*; as well as more conceptual; innovative and forward planning* – surely a sign of the times.

As regards leadership styles, when compared to the norms for managers and
professionals, heads were (at the 1 per cent level) not unsurprisingly significantly
more 'participatory' and 'consultative' in their preferred styles. Also, their preferences indicated heads to be more 'delegative'. These issues are discussed further
in Section 4 of this chapter.

Team types are derived from the work of Belbin (1981; see Table 3.2) and are
as follows. Heads proved significantly (at the 1 per cent level) more inclined to
prefer team roles of: 'coordinator'; 'plant' and 'resource investigator'. This does
not elicit surprise since these roles impinge directly upon major aspects of the
head's job, e.g. as 'chair', as a source of original ideas as innovator, and also in the
resource investigator mode, that is as the person who is forging relationships out
of the school on the school's behalf.

It is possible to draw attention to the fact that sustained differences between
the preferred work behaviours of headteachers when compared to the 'norm' for
managers and professionals appear to exist. These clearly identify that strengths
in managing people, and tasks, and that communication skills in order to work

Table 3.4: OPQ Concept 5.2: Mean response of headteachers plotted against managerial/professional norms

Low 1	2	3	4	5	6	7	8	9	High 10	RELATIONSHIPS WITH PEOPLE
					X					**Persuasive** – Enjoys selling, changes opinions of others, convincing with arguments, negotiates
						X				**Controlling** – Takes charge, directs, manages, organizes, supervises others **Assertive**
					X					**Independent** – Has strong views on things, difficult to manage, speaks up, argues, dislikes ties
					X					**Outgoing** – Fun loving, humorous, sociable, vibrant, talkative, jovial
					X					**Affiliative** – Has many friends, enjoys being in groups, likes companionship, shares things with friends **Gregarious**
					X					**Socially confident** – Puts people at ease, knows what to say, good with words
				X						**Modest** – Reserved about achievements, avoids talking about self, accepts others, avoids trappings of status
						X				**Democratic** – Encourages others to contribute, consults, listens and refers to others **Empathy**
					X					**Caring** – Considerate to others, helps those in need, sympathetic, tolerant
1	2	3	4	5	6	7	8	9	10	THINKING STYLES
				X						**Practical** – Down-to-earth, likes repairing and mending things, better with the concrete
					X					**Data rational** – Good with data, operates on facts, enjoys assessing and measuring
						X				**Artistic** – Appreciates culture, shows artistic flair, sensitive to visual arts and music **Fields of use**
						X				**Behavioural** – Analyzes thoughts and behaviour, psychologically minded, likes to understand people
			X							**Traditional** – Preserves well proven methods, prefers the orthodox, disciplined, conventional
					X					**Change oriented** – Enjoys doing new things, seeks variety, prefers novelty to routine, accepts changes **Abstract**
						X				**Conceptual** – Theoretical, intellectually curious, enjoys the complex and abstract
					X					**Innovative** – Generates ideas, shows ingenuity, thinks up solutions
						X				**Forward planning** – Prepares well in advance, enjoys target setting, forecasts trends, plans projects
				X						**Detail conscious** – Methodical, keeps things neat and tidy, precise, accurate **Structure**
				X						**Conscientious** – Sticks to deadlines, completes jobs, perseveres with routine, likes fixed schedules

Table 3.4:   (cont.)

Low 1	2	3	4	STENS 5	6	7	8	High 9	10	FEELINGS AND EMOTIONS
				X						**Relaxed** – Calm, relaxed, cool under pressure, free from anxiety, can switch off **Anxieties**
					X					**Worrying** – Worry when things go wrong, keyed-up before important events, anxious to do well
				X						**Tough minded** – Difficult to hurt or upset, can brush off insults, unaffected by unfair remarks
					X					**Emotional control** – Restrained in showing emotions, keeps feelings back, avoids outbursts **Controls**
						X				**Optimistic** – Cheerful, happy, keeps spirits up despite setbacks
				X						**Critical** – Good at probing the facts, sees the disadvantages, challenges assumptions
					X					**Active** – Has energy, moves quickly, enjoys physical exercise, doesn't sit still
					X					**Competitive** – Plays to win, determined to beat others, poor loser
					X					**Achieving** – Ambitious, sets sights high, career centred, results orientated **Energies**
					X					**Decisive** – Quick at conclusions, weighs things up rapidly, may be hasty, takes risks
				X						**Social desirability response** – Has tended to respond in a socially desirable way

Mean headteachers response = X
Mean for managers/professionals = STEN of 5.5

effectively beyond the immediate boundary of the school are all very necessary for performance of the head's job.

One possible use of an overarching personality 'profile' of heads is in a 'profile matching' exercise where an individual's profile is compared to the 'mean' profile for heads and his or her suitability for the job assessed. It is speculated that the mean or average personality profile of the people in an occupation is a guide to the ideal pattern of behaviour, since the individuals who have moved into the occupation and remained there are those that are well suited to the occupation.

Profile matching however has a number of drawbacks. There is no indication of the effectiveness of the 'mean profile'; it merely informs us that individuals of such profile have adjusted to the demands of the job because they choose to remain in the job. The mean profile may also be discriminatory; for example, if it is based on a male dominated sample of job holders. The worth of such personality profiles however lies in their contribution to the debate as to which personality characteristics are important in underpinning headteacher job performance, and their subsequent use in informing headteacher recruitment, management development and training.

Variations According to Gender of Headteacher

Some previous research and the literature on gender and headship would tend to indicate that male and female heads behave in different ways in managing their schools (Jones 1987; Gray 1987; Adler *et al*. 1993; Ozga 1993; Shakeshaft 1993). Much of this work argues that female heads adopt a less hierarchical and more democratic style of leadership. Jones (1987) observed the tendency by female heads to show more skill in motivating their staff and involving staff in shared tasks compared to the male heads in her sample. Shakeshaft (1987), in reviewing studies of male and female school leaders and their administrative styles, has focused on the areas of relationships, teaching and learning, and community. Women are depicted as communicating more and spending larger amounts of time with other people; as establishing more effective instructional processes; and building communities by an emphasis on a democratic and participative style that encourages inclusiveness.

In addition to differences in working style, it has also been suggested that the female head is perceived by others quite differently from the male head; for example, she is preferred by teachers to take on the role of 'facilitator' as opposed to the more male oriented 'coordinator' function (Johnston 1986). These issues are discussed at greater length later in this chapter.

To investigate the effect of gender upon headteachers' preferences in behaviour, team roles and leadership styles, the personality data was subjected to statistical analysis. Independent sample t-tests were applied to all personality dimensions by gender, including team types and leadership styles derived by SHL from weighted combinations of single personality scales. The t-values for OPQ dimensions, team types and leadership styles achieving significance levels of $p<0.01$ and $p<0.05$ are shown in Appendix 2. The findings are summarized below.

Female heads compared to their male counterparts, describe themselves as more:

- affiliative,
- democratic,
- caring,
- artistic,
- behavioural,
- detail conscious,
- conscientious, and
- worrying.

Additionally they tend to prefer the team roles of:

- team worker, and
- completer, and the leadership styles of
- participative leader, and
- consultative leader.

Male heads, in comparison with their female colleagues, characterize themselves as more:

- data rational,
- relaxed,

- tough minded,
- active, and
- competitive.

While they display no particular preference in team roles, in comparison to female heads they show a greater affinity to adopt the leadership style of a delegative leader.

Some of these findings are reflected in the large-scale standardization study conducted by Saville and Holdsworth (1992) on the general population, using the OPQ Concept 5.2, as mentioned earlier. A comparison of the gender differences found in the SHL study with those variations revealed with headteachers according to gender has led to the formulation of a number of hypotheses, discussed below.

Some gender differences between headteachers are likely to reflect stereotypical assumptions of male and female roles. Saville and Holdsworth Ltd have also reported a tendency by men in the general population sample to describe themselves as more data rational, relaxed, tough minded, active and competitive than do women, with the exception of delegative leader.

Gender differences reflected in the sample of headteachers which indicated that female heads saw themselves as more democratic, caring, and artistic, are also shown for women is SHL's standardization study of the general population. Also, the propensity for women to adopt to a greater extent than men the team roles of team worker and completer (Saville and Holdsworth 1993a) seems to be a factor generally applicable to women in the general population, including headteachers.

Thus there are a number of gender differences common to both the study on headteachers and the SHL Standardization study using a sample from the general population. These may be indicative of deep-seated stereotyped assumptions about men and women and their respective roles at work and in society.

There are gender differences found in the general population but not exhibited by headteachers. The men in the SHL sample, in addition to expressing a greater predilection than the women to adopt the behaviours shown above, also characterized themselves as more controlling, practical, innovative, and achieving than the females in the study. These latter gender differences were not however revealed in the headteachers' data.

Female heads, it seems, see themselves to be just as controlling in managing their schools as their male colleagues 'in directing and organizing others, issuing instructions and in taking charge of situations'. Allied to this, in terms of leadership style SHL's findings for the general population showed that directive leadership seemed to be significantly selected by men as opposed to women (Saville and Holdsworth 1994). Contrary to this finding, no significant differences were demonstrated by male and female headteachers on directive leadership. It is possible that the need to be directive, defined here as the maintenance of responsibility for planning and control, the issuing of instructions etc., represents an obligatory part of the headteacher's job regardless of favoured leadership or management style. Female headteachers, by comparison with their male counterparts, also expressed an equal preference to engage in practical activities as well as to be innovative in generating novel and creative ways of doing things.

While describing themselves as less competitive – a finding also reflected in the general population – female headteachers, unlike women in the SHL general population study, tend to describe themselves to be as achieving as their male equivalents. It seems that female heads have identified the need to set high goals for themselves, be career-centred, and ambitious, without manifesting the accompanying competitive drive, distinguishing many of their male colleagues.

There are contrasts between male and female headteachers in terms of behaviour preferences and leadership styles. Some significant variations between male and female headteachers and preferred job behaviours and leadership styles have emerged which are not shown in the SHL general population study. There appear to be some differences between male and female headteachers attributable to significant differences in the way that male and female heads claim to perform job tasks, and relate to, and involve, other people in school. For example, female headteachers describe themselves to be far more affiliative than their male colleagues. They tend to markedly prefer to work in groups, to share tasks and to be with others. They would also regard themselves as being detail conscious, favouring methodical work with a focus on orderliness, precision and accuracy, and conscientious in adhering to deadlines and fixed schedules, and in persevering with tedious and routine tasks.

These differences in behaviour preference are paralleled in heads' favoured team roles and leadership styles. For example the detail conscious and conscientious dimensions are indicative of the greater female tendency to adopt a team role of completer.

One of the most striking findings is the strong indication by female heads compared to their male equivalents of their preference to adopt the leadership styles of consultative leader and participative leader (see Figures 3.1 and 3.2). Female heads claim a preference for a style of leadership which favours consensus decision making; seeking the involvement of all relevant colleagues thereby securing their commitment and motivation; and a warm and friendly social style. These heads, while favouring the democratic approach, are also concerned with task accomplishment and are prepared to make decisions which are not always consensual but based on a personal analysis of all perspectives. These findings are not replicated, at least not to the extent shown with headteachers, in the population as a whole; SHL have found only a small difference in the general population between men and women on participative leadership and no differences have emerged for consultative leadership. The above would also fit with the tendency described earlier for women, including headteachers, to embrace the team role of team worker, to be a good listener who builds on others' ideas and promotes team harmony.

Conversely the male headteachers in this sample would seem to show a significant tendency as compared to the female heads to adopt a leadership style which is delegative (see Figure 3.3).

Delegative leaders believe in delegation of tasks and responsibility. They tend to communicate less with their staff and are inclined not to give clearly defined instructions or plan the work of the personnel they oversee. Such leaders tend not to seek the staffs' views as to how projects should be conducted, but are inclined simply to hand over the work to be done.

Figure 3.1: *Distribution of STEN scores for male and female heads on consultative leadership*

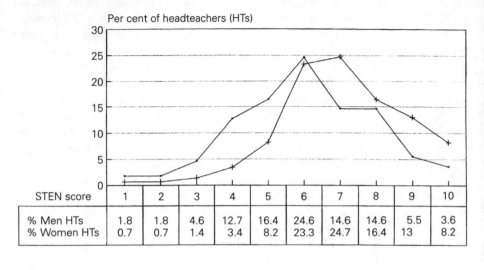

Per cent of headteachers (HTs)

STEN score	1	2	3	4	5	6	7	8	9	10
% Men HTs	1.8	1.8	4.6	12.7	16.4	24.6	14.6	14.6	5.5	3.6
% Women HTs	0.7	0.7	1.4	3.4	8.2	23.3	24.7	16.4	13	8.2

—•— % Men HTs   —+— % Women HTs

Figure 3.2: *Distribution of STEN scores for male and female heads on participative leadership*

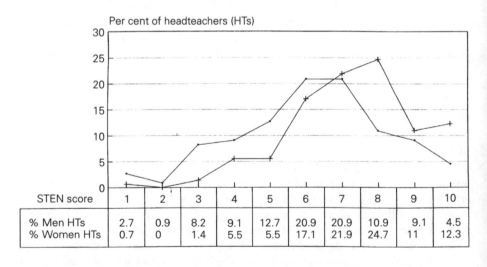

Per cent of headteachers (HTs)

STEN score	1	2	3	4	5	6	7	8	9	10
% Men HTs	2.7	0.9	8.2	9.1	12.7	20.9	20.9	10.9	9.1	4.5
% Women HTs	0.7	0	1.4	5.5	5.5	17.1	21.9	24.7	11	12.3

—•— % Men HTs   —+— % Women HTs

Figure 3.3:   Distribution of STEN scores for male and female heads on delegative leadership

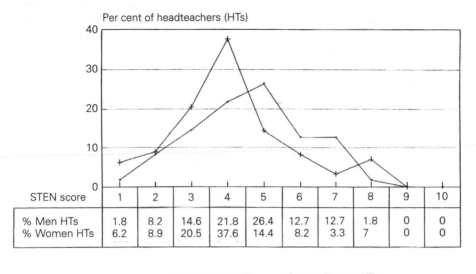

STEN score	1	2	3	4	5	6	7	8	9	10
% Men HTs	1.8	8.2	14.6	21.8	26.4	12.7	12.7	1.8	0	0
% Women HTs	6.2	8.9	20.5	37.6	14.4	8.2	3.3	7	0	0

——— % Men HTs   —+— % Women HTs

The Influence of School Sector/Phase

It has been suggested by Gray (1987) that, by and large, headteachers of primary and secondary schools have the personal qualities that characterize and distinguish their types of schools. The heads of primary schools are portrayed as displaying the 'feminine' aspects of personality, for example, the attributes of caring, tolerance, non-competitiveness, intuition etc. Secondary heads however, are described in terms of more 'masculine' qualities such as competitive, disciplined, highly regulated and formal.

The influence of school sector on headteachers' preferred personality dimensions has been investigated in the present research. The conduct of one-way analysis of variance measures on OPQ data has enabled us to determine the extent of similarities and differences, if any, between heads working in the primary sectors with those functioning in the secondary sector. A table showing the respective F-ratios for significant one-way analysis of variance measures is presented in Appendix 3.

Few significant differences were revealed between primary and secondary heads on OPQ dimensions. The relatively small number of significant differences are: secondary headteachers describe themselves as more data rational; conscientious; competitive; and achieving, and additionally show a greater predilection to adopt a team role of implementer. Conversely junior and primary, and in particular infant/first heads, seem much more inclined than their secondary colleagues to adopt the role of team worker.

Differences portrayed above between primary and secondary heads should however be interpreted with caution since they may be the artefact of a sample biased in terms of gender. Considerable efforts were made in conducting the research to control for sample bias. The research sample is however broadly skewed towards males in the secondary sector and females in the primary sector. This is a reflection of a national trend which shows that the secondary sector is staffed largely by male headteachers. Indeed it has been shown that the percentage of female secondary headteachers in an individual LEA can be as low as 5 per cent or less, although strong regional variations exist (see Edwards and Lyons 1994). The proportion of female secondary heads participating in the research is however higher at 30 per cent than the national ratio, which is usually quoted to be around the 15–20 per cent mark.

Differences reported here between school sector and the personality measures of data rational, competitive, and the team role dimension of team worker may be attributable to gender and the behaviour preferences of male and female headteachers rather than school sector. For example, the tendency for secondary heads to appear more competitive than primary heads may be a result of a secondary sample which is skewed towards males, who in turn describe themselves as being significantly more competitive than their female equivalents (as discussed in the earlier section on gender differences).

There are then a few variations according to school sector which have emerged and do not seem to be influenced by gender but may be characteristic of differences between primary and secondary heads and how they perceive themselves and their jobs. This would include the dimension of achieving with secondary heads in the sample depicting themselves to be significantly higher than those in the primary sectors on the need to be ambitious, to set one's targets high and to be career-centred. Secondary heads in this sample would seem to show a greater predilection than the primary heads to adopt the team role of implementer, the capacity to turn decisions and strategies into manageable tasks and to bring logical and methodical pursuit of objectives to the team.

Three important caveats need to be put forward at this point. The substantiation of all claims requires further rigorous research conducted with a carefully constructed sample. It would be unwise without corroborative evidence to draw any firm conclusions. As with all significant differences between groups, variance in OPQ scores amongst individuals within a group far outweighs any variance that may appear to exist between groups; although a few differences have arisen the picture that has emerged is one in which there is a far greater number of similarities than dissimilarities in the personality profiles of primary and secondary headteachers.

School sector and leadership style

A comparison of the leadership styles of primary males against secondary males, and primary females against secondary females has examined headteachers' leadership styles, where gender was kept constant and sector was the independent variable. This analysis noted there were no significant differences between the leadership styles adopted by primary and secondary sector heads. That is, both males in primary and males in secondary for example show an equal preference to adopt all available leadership styles; no one style characterizes a particular school sector.

Only one exception to this was found, female heads in secondary schools seem to describe themselves as significantly more directive in leadership style than female primary heads. This may be a reflection of essential differences between the sectors in terms of school size and organizational structure.

Summary and Conclusions

The findings from the Occupational Personality Questionnaire lead us towards a number of tentative assumptions. It would also be wise to bear in mind however that the questionnaire utilized is a self-report instrument and represents headteachers' declarations about their own behaviour and personal leadership style which may not always be congruent with others' perceptions of the heads' behaviour.

The findings from the OPQ indicate that:

- There is far greater variance *between* individual headteachers in their OPQ scores, but there do appear to be some common features in heads' choice of behaviours and leadership styles. These attributes – for example the preference to be democratic, consultative, and participatory, but at the same time controlling etc. – are suggestive of attributes characterizing *all* headteachers, distinguishing heads from other managerial and professional positions.
- There are some gender differences between headteachers likely to be a manifestation of stereotyped images of men and women in work and society.
- Some gender differences displayed amongst men and women in the general population are not found amongst headteachers.
- There are some contrasts in the behaviour and leadership preferences of male and female headteachers, particularly in the way they relate to and involve other people in school. While all heads would generally tend towards participatory and consultative behaviour, female heads claim to have a greater preference than their male colleagues to adopt the styles of consultative leader and participative leader. Male heads would in turn appear to show a greater preference for the style of delegative leader.
- Few differences were revealed in the behaviours and leadership styles favoured by primary and secondary headteachers. Thus the majority of dissimilarities observed are likely to be a reflection of gender differences between male and female heads and their preferred ways of managing, rather than being attributable to a fundamental distinction in the way primary and secondary schools are organized and run.

Section 2: The Work Profiling System (WPS)

The WPS questionnaire represents an integrated job analysis system providing a sophisticated means for the collection and analysis of job task, job context and behavioural information. It represents one approach to be used along with other approaches in order to undertake a comprehensive job analysis.

The WPS essentially collects task and behaviour-orientated job information and then uses a statistical process to infer the required human attributes for successful performance of the job. The basis underpinning this approach was provided for SHL by a panel of experienced occupational psychologists in which required attributes were linked to task statements on the basis of rigorously scrutinized judgments. Methods of assessment are then linked directly to the specified attributes and their relevance for assessment calculated depending on two factors:

- the efficiency with which the method accurately assesses the target attribute; and
- the overall importance of the target attribute to the analyzed job.

WPS information is computer analyzed to:

- provide a profile of job tasks and context;
- specify a profile of human attributes required for effective job performance; and
- identify relevant assessment methods and/or training requirements.

Validity and Reliability of the WPS

Support for the validity of the WPS, that is the extent to which the description of the job produced by the WPS accurately reflects the actual job, has come from an independent study conducted by Huba and Melchior (1989). Reliability coefficients for the WPS are high (Saville and Holdsworth 1990b) (see Table 3.5).

Table 3.5: Reliability of the Work Profiling System

Work Profiling System		Median Test-Retest Reliability Coefficient
Part 1	Importance Scale	0.73
	Time Scale	0.71
Part 2	All Context items	0.66

Source: Saville and Holdsworth 1990b

Structure of the Questionnaire

The WPS questionnaire is divided into two parts. The first part concerns job tasks, the second part job context factors. Job tasks are organized into seven overarching task sections, which in turn are further divided into 31 task categories. This information is set out in Table 3.6. Each task category identifies one page of the

Table 3.6: WPS structure of task 'sections'

Section	Task Category	Specific Tasks (Number of question items per task category)
A	Managing tasks	
	1 Planning	14
	2 Implementing/coordinating	8
	3 Controlling/directing	10
	4 Reviewing/evaluating	13
B	Managing people	
	1 Supervising/directing	14
	2 Appraising/evaluating/developing	14
	3 Motivating	14
	4 Assisting/caring	13
	5 Disciplining/disputes/grievances	13
	6 Counselling	6
	7 Cooperating/liaising	8
C	Receiving information	
	1 Investigating/observing/searching	14
	2 Taking information from the senses	11
D	Thinking creatively	
	1 Artistic creativity	7
	2 Problem solving/designing	12
E	Working with information	
	1 Assessing/evaluating	14
	2 Analyzing/diagnosing	11
	3 Integrating/coding/estimating	14
	4 Calculating	12
	5 Interpreting	7
	6 Checking	8
	7 Deciding	9
	8 Learning/researching	10
F	Communicating	
	1 Influencing/advising	11
	2 Presenting/instructing/briefing	9
	3 Informing/discussing/interviewing	13
	4 Writing/administering	10
	5 Representing/selling	12
	6 Public relations/developing relationships	11
G	Physical	
	1 Performing physical tasks/operating vehicles	11
	2 Using tools/machinery	12

(managerial/professional questionnaire (c) Saville and Holdsworth Ltd, 1990)

questionnaire containing a number of question items, called specific tasks. The number of specific tasks per task category can also be found in Table 3.6.

Part 2 of the WPS questionnaire relates to job context information. The following items are regarded as most relevant to the analysis reported here:

1 breadth of job related knowledge (the extent to which the job requires knowledge across functions, e.g. professional knowledge, personnel, budgeting, marketing, etc. within the organization);

2   levels of reporting (the number of reporting steps to the head of the organization within which the job falls);

3   demands of change (the extent to which the job is changing or presents new situations to be dealt with);

4   financial impact of performance (the likely total annual financial impact on the organization of inadequate performance by the job holder);

5   responsibility for resources (the annual value of organizational resources for which the job holder is responsible);

6   responsibility for personnel (the total number of personnel for which the job holder has direct or indirect responsibility);

7   interpersonal contact (who with and the frequency of interpersonal contact required by the job);

8   type of interpersonal contact (the mode and frequency of interpersonal contact required by the job);

9   specific accountabilities (the degree of importance to job objectives of specific types of accountability, e.g. budgets, equipment, quality matters, public relations, etc.);

10   time span of impact of errors (the average length of time it would take before errors made within the job would have an observable or measurable effect);

11   freedom to structure (the extent to which a job holder is free to structure the objectives and consequent activities of the job);

12   working hours (the number of hours usually worked in a week by a job holder).

Questionnaire Completion

For the questionnaire completion sessions heads were asked to meet together in a series of central locations in the various regions of England and Wales. Prior to the session they had been sent a list of the WPS task categories and were also asked to identify five to 10 current key job objectives. The atmosphere at the questionnaire completion sessions was deliberately as informal as possible. Heads were encouraged to discuss freely issues arising from questionnaire completion with other colleagues and with the researchers.

The first stage of questionnaire completion entailed respondents being asked to:

- work with sort cards to identify the task categories they regarded as important for meeting their job objectives to try to identify not more than eight to 10 task categories;
- each task category selected directed the respondent to a page of questions (specific tasks) relating to that task category found in the questionnaire booklet, and respondents answer only those questions that they feel are part of their jobs.

Participants respond to each question thus identified:

- first, on a seven point scale according to its importance in meeting their job objectives; and
- second, in terms of the amount of time spent on a weekly/monthly/annual basis.

Finally, for the first part of the WPS questionnaire respondents were asked to rank their selected task categories on a scale of 1 to 8 in terms of the importance of each task category to meeting their job objectives.

The data collection session ideally concludes with a one-to-one diagnostic (validation) interview with one of the researchers who (using the completed questionnaire and other allied information about the job) asks the head to talk through the items selected on the questionnaire. Question selection and task category ranking can be changed at this stage if the respondent wishes, though in practice this rarely proves necessary.

Analysis of Heads' Responses to Part One (Task Categories) of the WPS Questionnaire

In this section we shall be concerned with reporting the results of an analysis of job task and the corresponding time related management factors. While the central focus of the analysis here leads to a profile for all headteachers, some information relating to a subsidiary analysis of differences between heads' responses for the different school phases will also be reported.

For the initial stage of WPS analysis 99 headteachers were selected from our larger sample of 255 headteachers. The sampling criteria reflected the major variables of heads, that is: age, experience of headship, gender, etc. and the major school variables including: region and location, school phase, type of intake, etc. (the full details of sampling can be found at Appendix 1). However for later stages of statistical analysis the full sample of 255 headteachers was used.

For the analysis reported here a cut-off after the first 12 task categories selected by heads has been used, as numbers of heads selecting a task category tended to fall off rapidly after the twelfth item. The result of the initial analysis of task categories is shown in Table 3.7.

Task categories

That the task categories 'planning' and 'motivating' are ranked first and second neatly encapsulates the current problems and concerns of school management in England and Wales. Planning, which here includes managing the budget, has become of necessity a prime activity for heads as the head's accountabilities and responsibilities at school level consequent on the Education Acts have their impact. Motivating staff in a very difficult work and financial climate now is increasingly important and demanding of the head's time, as workloads on staff increase, as few

Table 3.7: Key job tasks

Rank Order	Task Category	Overarching task areas from which response is drawn	Specific Tasks	N = 99*
1	Planning	Managing tasks	Planning long term objectives Setting up financial budget Planning short term objectives	(97) (90) (97)
2	Motivating	Managing people	Creating a good team spirit Encouraging cooperation Gaining willing cooperation	(87) (85) (87)
3	Assisting/Caring	Managing people	Looking after needs of children Looking after emotional needs Assisting in learning difficulty	(53) (46) (34)
4	Appraising/Evaluating/Developing people	Managing people	Assessing needs of people Creating confidence Appraising for promotion/recruitment	(52) (65) (68)
5	Implementing/Coordinating	Managing tasks	Organizing resources Ensuring efficient coordination Allocating resources	(55) (55) (56)
6	Deciding	Working with information	Deciding action – with others Making decisions after evaluation Decisions affecting welfare, etc.	(58) (58) (58)
7	Controlling/Directing	Managing tasks	Controlling people resources Directing implementation of policy Ensuring agreements are adhered to	(44) (38) (40)
8	PR/Developing relationships	Communicating	Getting on well – team/unit Maintaining good PR Establishing network of contacts	(51) (57) (48)
9	Counselling	Managing people	Advising on improving job performance Counselling on personal problems Advising interpersonal behaviour	(49) (47) (44)
10	Influencing/Advising	Communicating	Advising governors Making a spoken case for action Arguing a case in formal meetings	(47) (49) (48)
11	Learning/Researching	Working with information	Keeping abreast of developments Learning new systems/methods, etc. Undertaking informal training	(40) (38) (39)
12	Assessing/Evaluating	Working with information	Evaluating output of the system Making a logical evaluation Evaluating alternatives	(13) (39) (34)

* Number of raters per specific task is displayed in brackets.

financial incentives are available to offer to staff and in fact as staff redundancies become increasingly common.

The appearance of 'assisting/caring' as the third ranked category reflects an occupational sector related choice, being one feature distinguishing the work of those who manage schools from most other occupational sectors.

Of the first six ranked task categories, two concern managing tasks and three managing people, with the sixth task category, 'deciding', drawn from the overarching task area of 'working with information.' From an examination of the ranked specific tasks a strong managing people orientation emerges as underpinning the selection of the latter task category. The headteacher's job has been changed by Education Acts and increasing financial and site-based management, so perhaps there should be few surprises in the task categories identified. With reference to the framework developed earlier in Chapter 2 on the relation between different job competencies (i.e. generic, occupational, organizational and individual) there were few surprises caused by the selection by our sample of these task categories.

There is a strong sense derived from the task categories selected by our head-teacher sample of tasks generic to the work of many managers. Assisting/caring appearing so high in the rankings is the exception. While controlling/directing also seems a natural aspect of the work of heads, its appearance selected as seventh highest task category does appear anomalous to much current management teaching to release 'value' in schools by increasing staff participation in the decision making process.

The overarching task area of 'communicating' is represented here by PR/ developing relationships and influencing/advising. The latter reflects the need for the head to influence others for the overall development of the school, particularly governors, while PR/developing relationships (not marketing), ranked eighth, is for schools a relatively *newly emerging* category at this level of importance. The task area 'working with information' is represented by assessing/evaluating and learning/ researching. Heads constantly need to collect and analyze information in order to monitor and evaluate what is occurring within the organization. Assessing/evalua-ting representing this orientation is selected as the twelfth category by this sample. Learning/researching again draws our attention to the rate of change imposed upon the educational system in England and Wales and the need for heads to remain upon a steep upward learning curve to stay abreast of new developments, and also to influence the development of their schools proactively.

The job as represented by these responses seems to be about: managing tasks, managing people, working with information in order to make decisions about tasks and people and communicating these decisions. There is not one key focus to the job. It is complex, entails considerable skill and professional expertise in sector-specific task areas, requires a high order of interpersonal skills and awareness and, because of the rapid rate of change, requires a continuous personal orientation to the head's own growth and development.

Time management

As part of the completion of the questionnaire heads were asked to identify first those 'specific tasks' which they regarded as most important to meeting their ob-jectives for the school, and second, to provide an estimate of the time spent on the activity. Most time is spent upon the identified specific tasks because they are the most important, not that they are perceived as the most important because most

Table 3.8:   Time management

Most important items: ranked
Planning long term objectives
Planning short term objectives
Creating a good team spirit
Setting up financial budget
Encouraging cooperation
Gaining willing cooperation
Revising plans due to change
Defining objectives

Most time-consuming items: ranked
Creating a good team spirit
Planning short term objectives
Looking after needs of children
Planning long term objectives
Encouraging cooperation
Setting up financial budget
Understanding others' needs/motives
Formulating or adjusting policy

time is spent on them. There is considerable overlap between specific tasks most frequently identified as being most important and those identified as most time consuming, although some slight change in order of ranking does occur (see Table 3.8).

The specific tasks listed here reflect current concerns and problems encountered by heads and convey a clear flavour of the day to day issues that heads are dealing with. The most important items are 'planning long and short term objectives', 'setting up a financial budget', 'defining objectives' and 'revising plans due to change'; also, reflecting so well current staff issues, 'encouraging cooperation' and 'gaining willing cooperation'. The most time consuming items are some also ranked as most important, 'creating a good team spirit', 'planning short term objectives', 'planning long term objectives', 'encouraging cooperation' and 'setting up a financial budget'. The specific tasks identified here as most time consuming and not earlier identified under the 'importance' priorities are 'looking after needs of children', 'understanding others' needs/motives' and 'formulating or adjusting policy'. There would seem to be little doubt about the importance of these specific tasks for effective training and for successful performance of headship.

Differences between Primary and Secondary Schools on Selection and Ranking of Task Categories

Earlier it was mentioned that a subsidiary analysis had been undertaken of task category selection and ranking where responses of primary and secondary heads had been compared. Here we use subsamples of primary schools (N = 97) and secondary schools (N = 51) to report this analysis. The one self-evident overall finding to emerge from this analysis is that similarities in task selection and ranking

Table 3.9: Significant differences between primary and secondary headteachers in task category selection

Task Category	Pearson Chi Values (p < 0.05; d.f.1)	
	P > S	S > P
Managing tasks, Implementing/Coordinating	10.35	
Managing people, Assisting/Caring	42.78	
Working with information, Checking	5.49	
Working with information, Learning/Researching	6.50	
Managing people, Supervising/Directing		6.19
Communicating, Influencing/Advising		25.30

P = primary schools (N = 97)
S = secondary schools (N = 51)

are infinitely greater than dissimilarities. However some dissimilarities are found (see Table 3.9).

The more extensively hierarchical organization of secondary schools, larger in unit size and with far greater numbers of staff, probably entails a lessened immediacy of direct contact between head and pupils, and head with staff and other adults. Greater immediacy of contact with the primary head is likely because of a more flattened hierarchical structure and fewer staff in the school; even the school secretary is probably part time. In these circumstances, the primary head is likely to have a more direct and hands-on involvement than might be the case for the secondary head. Secondary heads show a greater preference for 'supervising/directing', and primary heads attach greater importance to the 'assisting/caring' dimension and to 'checking' than do their secondary counterparts.

In this sample secondary heads place a greater reliance on a system where 'implementing and coordinating functions' are (locally) delegated within the school. In the primary sector it seems that this task is more likely to rest with the head. The secondary head also places greater emphasis upon 'influencing and advising'. This is a communicating task category which would involve the head in such matters as presenting a case, negotiating, defending a position or procedure, policy, etc. and certainly where contact with significant figures outside of the school is likely to be involved and, of course, with the chair of governors.

Conversely, primary heads indicated 'learning and researching' as a prioritized task category. Generally speaking we found that primary heads in our sample had been involved in local and financial management of their schools for a shorter period of time than had their secondary colleagues. This may well account for the prioritization.

Key Context Factors for Primary and Secondary Schools

In Part 2 of the WPS questionnaire heads were asked to reflect upon those context items which have an important bearing upon their work. Many of these context factors would dictate how and where task categories are performed, the nature of the head's involvement and the aspect(s) of the task category which is actually prioritized and undertaken.

In order to perform the job effectively, the breadth of job related knowledge is regarded by heads as substantial across all functions. Heads from primary and secondary schools see the job itself as undergoing basic change. It would seem necessary therefore, first, that anyone who wishes successfully to discharge headship functions must anticipate coping with ongoing change in the educational environment, and second, that he or she must recognize that headship is itself undergoing a substantial transformation.

Heads in primary schools assert that they have a *moderate* amount of freedom to structure the objectives and consequent activities of the job. That is, they would anticipate receiving instructions concerning general schedules and work targets but have the freedom to adapt and to innovate. Whereas secondary headteachers claim that they have *much* freedom, needing to conform to policy guidelines only, but within which there is considerable latitude for determining action. Here we begin therefore to identify those key context items which indicate essential differences between the job of primary head and that of the secondary headteacher.

Consequent upon this is the time span of 'impact of errors', that is, if the head makes a mistake within their job then how long would it be before it shows up by having some observable or measurable effect? For primary schools this would fall into a one to four week time span. However, for the secondary heads, the impact of error falls between one to three months.

For primary heads, the annual value of the organizational resources for which the job holder is responsible (for example salaries, wages, operating costs, etc.) generally falls between £100,000 and £499,000. In the case of the secondary head the figure on average lies between £1 million and £1.9 million. For both primary and secondary heads the financial impact on the organization of inadequate performance by the head is perceived as a large impact involving tens of thousands of pounds.

The total numbers of personnel managed including both supervisory and non-supervisory staff are considerably larger in the secondary school. The hierarchical organizational structure typically found in secondary schools means however that those who directly report to the head, reported as being on average between six and ten staff in this study, is the same as in the primary sector. There are however some differences as to the range of individuals dealt with, the range of issues likely to be occurring, and the level of detail involved when comparison is made between sectors.

The above is illustrated in the interpersonal contact that the respective positions entail. For primary heads, moderate interpersonal contact, involving between 10 and 20 per cent of the head's time is respectively spent working with staff at senior management, administrative, supervisory, middle management and junior management levels, as well as with the general public.

For secondary heads a different picture immediately emerges in that here the heads perceive that they have frequent interpersonal contact, that is over 20 per cent of their time, with senior management staff, and moderate contact (10–20 per cent of time) with middle management and administrative staff. They describe having only occasional contact with junior management and supervisory staff, students, the general public, manual work force, and trade union representatives.

Heads from both sectors carry high specific accountabilities for the standards staff bring to their work, the quality of the work produced, and for public relations. Heads on average claim to be working approximately 61 hours per week.

From the analysis so far the picture is emerging of the secondary school – larger in unit size, consisting of greater numbers of both teaching and non-teaching staff, with a more extensive hierarchical organizational structure, with responsibility for greater resources and greater freedom of action in policy matters – which begins to indicate how the job of running a secondary school differs from managing the usually smaller primary school. (It is however acknowledged that there are many primary schools which are of equivalent size and some even bigger than many of the smaller secondary schools.)

Evidence from the task analysis of the WPS also supports this view. The identification of the task category of supervising/directing by the secondary heads, and variation in specific tasks, such as the need in secondary schools to set up administrative systems and allocate duties to others more formally, as well as the greater need to attend to staffing issues such as promotion and recruitment, are cases in point and tend to bear out these differences.

The generally smaller primary school, with fewer members of staff and a correspondingly increased immediacy of access to headteachers, implies the head's likely and predictable direct hands-on involvement in most aspects of the work of the school. Smaller numbers of staff and a flatter hierarchical structure may increase the opportunity of staff to participate directly in many aspects of managing the school. Alternatively, it may lead to the head in a much more traditional mode of headship, taking on an increased workload in order to protect staff from unnecessary intrusion by enabling them to concentrate on their teaching and other professional duties.

Summary

We have used a technique of job analysis using a structured questionnaire, widely used in other employment sectors in the UK, to collect data from a sample of 255 heads in the maintained schools sector. These returns were subsequently analyzed via computer analysis, initially using a subsample of 99 heads, to determine similarity and dissimilarity in job task and job context related areas. The technique used has enabled a focus to be made across the head's functions rather than concentrating specifically on those necessary aspects which fall into the professional and technical domains.

Overall it seems that the similarities between primary and secondary schools are greater than the dissimilarities, both in terms of task categories and specific tasks chosen, and the rankings assigned to these. Heads from all sectors would seem to engage in, for example, planning, motivating, implementing/coordinating, appraising/evaluating/developing people, deciding, and controlling/directing.

There is a great deal of agreement amongst heads as to the most important and most time consuming activities they regularly undertake. These well reflect the current pressures and difficulties that they regularly face and must attempt to resolve, often in circumstances where a fully satisfactory resolution is not achievable.

Prioritization of headteacher training needs almost becomes self-evident. Those needs are key task areas which fall into the professional and technical domain: defining objectives, setting up the budget, planning long and short term objectives. Those matters calling for personal strength or resolve should also be included, such as revising plans due to change and formulating or adjusting policy. Those activities which call upon considerable interpersonal skills are keenly represented in the head's key activities and reflect so well the difficult circumstances heads regularly face – encouraging cooperation, gaining willing cooperation, creating a good team spirit, and understanding others' needs or motives. Not least within this prioritization of course is 'looking after the needs of children'.

Further similarity is highlighted in the job context factors described by heads of all sectors; for example all heads perceive the need for a considerable breadth of job related knowledge, and recognize that the job itself is undergoing basic change.

The large degree of commonality of management activity between those heads working in primary and secondary schools appears an issue of substance when matters concerning recruitment and training/development of heads are considered. However, while there is to a large extent similarity in the management tasks identified by primary and secondary heads, differences necessarily do occur. There is evidence that secondary heads place greater emphasis than do their primary colleagues on influencing/advising and PR/developing relationships, indicating that at the time of this data collection they had more actively embraced the need in the extant climate to maintain favourable public relations with parents, the local community and governors.

On the other hand primary heads identify preferences for task categories which are not shown by their secondary colleagues. For example learning and researching is a prioritized task category, and it is hypothesized that this was due to their more recent involvement in local management of schools (LMS) at the time of sampling.

Primary heads also indicated greater frequency of choice of the task category assisting/caring although this may be due to gender effects (see the discussion on gender differences for the OPQ). It is likely to reflect the more direct and personal involvement by the heads of these schools with all staff, other adults and pupils, an aspect not necessarily featuring in the work of the secondary head, where the head is likely to be more distanced from contact with many staff and pupils, through the more extensive hierarchical staffing structure.

It would appear from the analysis made of the work of this sample of heads, that the head's job is a blend of managing tasks, managing people, working with information to make decisions about these two elements and communicating these issues to aid the development of the school. There is not a key focus on any one element: it is diverse in its array of activities.

Previous research directs our attention to the pace and pressure under which the head operates; and to the brevity, discontinuity and face to face nature of many of the activities undertaken (Lyons 1974, 1976; Clerkin 1985). That schools are experiencing continuous change and severe resource constraint are also well documented. If these factors are taken together with the findings noted above, that the head's job is diverse in its array of activities, and that there is not a key focus on any one element, then it is evident that it is indeed a difficult job to do well.

The framework put forward earlier begins to help in identifying core elements of the job, those aspects that are occupational sector-specific, those that are organization-specific, and those that may have a large element of individuation attached. Such identification certainly helps in moving towards more effective training and by extrapolation to effective recruitment. The research implications are also large as a tentative basis begins to be laid for longitudinal research particularly leading to satisfying validity issues, and also for comparison to be made with the work of heads in other countries, with the work of managers in other occupational sectors, as well as with more detailed research within the wider schools sector. While individuation of headteacher performance and the needs of an individual school are always paramount, nevertheless some of the basic and necessary requirements of headship are reinforced through this analysis and enable comparison to be made of individual requirements against the generic profile being developed here.

We shall now use the information generated thus far to take the first step in the construction of a headteacher's profile comprising job description and the person specification necessary to manage the job task and job context factors effectively.

Section 3: The Headteacher's Job Description and Person Specification

The purpose in undertaking a job analysis of the headteacher position is to collect in a sophisticated and structured manner information which will provide an accurate description of key job tasks that the head undertakes and to construct a clear picture of the context in which the head performs his or her work. Then, from the analysis of job task and job context information and behavioural information, identify the personal skills that are of critical importance for the successful performance of the head's job.

The data also provides a means for the generation and validation of management competencies. This is discussed further in Chapter 4. While an indicative job description is presented below, this can be admittedly no more than a guide to key issues in determining the job description and allied person specification which may arise and be necessary in any particular school.

It is likely that job descriptions would conform to the framework discussed earlier for competencies (see Figure 2.7). That is, they would be composed of elements which appear to be generic to most managerial positions. Second, that strong occupational sector-specific criteria are also to the fore, and third, that some considerable individuation occurring either through school-determined or individual needs would also be present in any actual job description that applies to a particular head in a particular school.

Indicative Job Description

Job Title:	Headteacher
School And Location:	St. John's School, Midtown
Salary Range:	Group . . . .
Reports To:	Governing Body
Main Purpose of Job:	To manage the overall school activities to ensure first class educational provision to pupils, their families and the wider community.
Job Objectives:	<ul><li>To meet the needs of the community by setting standards for the school that comply with the requirements of current legislation and the implementation of policies adopted by governors.</li><li>To provide and to monitor a budget for the school in order to maximize the use of resources.</li><li>To provide and communicate a view of best practice for the school to adopt that is in line with current OFSTED inspection criteria.</li><li>To motivate and mobilize others to maximize their personal and professional development in order to facilitate ongoing organizational change and development.</li><li>To keep abreast of new educational and management developments for the purposes of personal growth and school renewal.</li><li>To maintain high visibility for the school within the local community and generate additional revenue for school projects.</li></ul>

Special Requirements
(as necessary)

Key Tasks and Activities

The main task areas and their associated principal activities – given in rank order of importance – for the job role are:

1 **Planning**
Planning long term objectives
Setting up financial budget
Planning short term objectives

2 **Motivating**
Creating a good team spirit
Encouraging cooperation
Gaining willing cooperation

3 **Assisting/Caring**
Looking after needs of children
Looking after emotional needs
Assisting in learning difficulty

4 **Appraising/Evaluating**
Assessing needs of people
Creating confidence
Appraising for promotion/
recruitment

5 **Implementing/Coordinating**
Organizing resources
Ensuring efficient coordination
Allocating resources

6 **Deciding**
Deciding action – with others
Making decisions after evaluation
Decisions affecting welfare, etc.

7 **Controlling/Directing**
Controlling people resources
Directing implementation of
policy

Ensuring agreements adhered to

8 **PR/Developing relationships**
Getting on well with team/unit
Maintaining good PR
Establishing a network of
contacts

9 **Counselling**
Advising to improve job
performance
Counselling on personal
problems
Advising on interpersonal
behaviour

10 **Influencing/Advising**
Advising governors
Making a spoken case for action
Arguing a case in formal
meetings

11 **Learning/Researching**
Keeping abreast of
developments
Learning new systems/methods,
etc.
Undertaking informal training

12 **Assessing/Evaluating**
Evaluating output of the system
Making a logical evaluation
Evaluating alternatives

Key Context Factors

1 **Breadth of job-related knowledge**
Substantial across functions

2 **Level of reporting**
Head of organization

3 **Demands of change**
Job undergoing basic change

4 **Financial impact of performance**
Large: £10,000

5 **Responsibility for resources**
£100,000–999,000

6 **Responsibility for personnel**
Total personnel: 21–50
Non-supervisory personnel: 11–20
Supervisory personnel: 6–10
Direct reports: 6–10

7 **Interpersonal contact**
Senior management level: Frequent, 20 per cent
Administrative staff: Moderate, 10–20 per cent
Middle management level: Moderate, 10–20 per cent
Junior management level: Moderate, 10–20 per cent
Supervisory level: Moderate, 10–20 per cent
General public: Moderate, 10–20 per cent

8 **Type of interpersonal contact**
Informing: Moderate, 10–20 per cent
Negotiating: Moderate, 10–20 per cent
Advising: Moderate, 10–20 per cent
Assessing: Moderate, 10–20 per cent
Directing: Moderate, 10–20 per cent
Persuading: Moderate, 10–20 per cent

9 **Specific accountabilities**
People standards: High
Product quality: High
Public relations: High
Work methods: High
Others' safety: High

10 **Time span of impact of errors**
Moderate term: 1 to 3 months

11 **Freedom to structure**
Much freedom: policy guide

Person Specification

The personal attributes required for the job of headteacher are:	
Education	Hons Degree
Job-related formal training	7–9 months
Job-related work experience	7–9 years

The most important abilities are:

Communication skills

Reason logically verbally and in writing

Is clear and expressive in written communication

Speaks in a clear and articulate manner

Number skills

Numeric reasoning

Calculates using simple formulae

Creative thinking skills

Generates varied ideas

Generates original ideas

Key

 Critical over a breadth of functions

Critical for some functions

Desirable

The most important personality attributes are:
Of critical importance applying to most functions
Enjoys forming short term plans Critically evaluates suggestions Enjoys strategic planning Uses data/logic in analyzing Confident with people Analyzes others' behaviour Sympathetic and tolerant
Of critical importance applying to many functions
Consults before decisions Takes an optimistic view Likes to be with groups Is ambitious for success Can sell ideas and be persuasive Does not always follow conventional approach
Of importance applying to a number of functions
Concerned with details Can switch off from work problems Directs/manages/controls others Keeps feelings hidden Enjoys working with theory Feelings are difficult to hurt Seeks change/variety in work Sees routine tasks through to end Generates creative ideas/solutions

The job description and person specification presented here are put forward as an indicative guide. The authors acknowledge the limitations of a 'generic' job description. However, for heads it can provide a useful framework for them to reflect upon aspects of their own job and perhaps to consider again areas of their jobs which the outline provides but which in their own case may not be sufficiently covered. For governors, initially it maps out key elements of the head's job to help them formulate, for example selection criteria and evaluate applicants' CVs. However, we would suggest that it provides a framework which should be revised or supplemented when the requirements of an individual school or individual head are considered.

The next section discusses some of the issues emerging from the research data and analysis up to this point.

Section 4: Difficulties and Dilemmas for the Head

The analysis we have undertaken of the headteacher's job, while still incomplete, is nevertheless of substance and is as accurate, as objective and as practicable as is possible to provide a basis upon which future research can be focused.

The tasks in the job make demands upon the headteacher that are contradictory and pull the individual in different directions. It is here that a detailed job analysis and information from a personality questionnaire provide detail and subtlety of interpretation. Without such information, action has to proceed based upon little more than informed guesswork.

Some of the issues that emerge from the analysis are dilemmas implicit in headship and for that matter to the work of managers in general; some are problems or practical difficulties which may or may not be amenable to training or resolvable at the time of recruitment; some may occur at the level of job-person match or mismatch, etc. Certainly we must always be ready to acknowledge that:

- the job and headship are undergoing fundamental and ongoing change, and necessarily anticipate that heads recruited or undergoing training now will be managing schools well into the next century, and that the criteria that we are presently advancing are themselves time-based;
- while raising these issues and with the resourcing immediately available to schools, we recognize that conflicting and unfulfillable demands will continue to be made upon headteachers.

Nevertheless heads continue to offer accessibility and the system tolerates their preparedness to use time in relatively mundane ways, typically when no one else is available and that they do so while logging on average a 61 hour working week. While this provides the ongoing operational context, it still remains essential for heads to recognize that they actually need to acquire and then use for organizational purposes new information and skills if they are to continue functioning as effective heads leading effective schools.

In Chapter 2 we drew attention to two of the theoretical models which underpin part of our research. That is, Boyatzis and Kolb's, 'Modes of growth and adaptation throughout career and life' (1992), and our classification of job tasks and competencies as generic, occupation-specific and organizationally or personally individuated. Complementary to these two frameworks is that proposed by Rosemary Stewart (1982) in *Choices for the Manager*, as constraints, demands and choices. These frameworks, amongst others drawn from the fields of management and organizational/occupational psychology, have guided our thinking.

We can note from the Boyatzis and Kolb model and from Rosemary Stewart that any individual leader is likely to be influenced by the development stage of their own career, by the stage of development of the organization, as well as by their own preferences in the way(s) in which they prefer to give leadership. If we therefore take these issues into account when examining training, development or recruitment needs, then certainly we would expect to find

- that over time the headteacher himself or herself will very probably change;
- that the gender of the head tracks, as shown by the responses of the sample, into preferred personality styles of working;
- that any aspect of training/development should be closely scrutinized in order to identify those aspects amenable to training, and those aspects which are much more difficult to influence or change by training when the fit between the (potential) head and the needs of the school are being considered.

It would also be our expectation that the head and the school would be constantly subject to the interacting forces of change. In this sample many heads have only held the one headship and have been in the same post for over 15 years.

Should Heads Focus More on Other Task Areas of Their Work?

The outcomes of the WPS survey have identified the critical importance of those matters of a school 'task' or 'professional nature', of the skills necessary to handle (all) 'managing people matters', to 'working with information', and to a lesser extent 'communicating'. Since the volume of reported activity falls into the task and working with people areas, is this perhaps at the expense of more time being allocated to 'communicating' and to 'working with information' than is presently reported and would schools be managed better if this were the case? A principal area of activity for managers in general is 'working with information'. This would appear to offer a more reflective approach to their job than sometimes appears the case for heads.

To this end we should also consider task categories not identified in the returns of this sample but which appear in other research returns. For example, the category 'thinking creatively' was identified on the WPS research returns by a sample of US elementary principals (Erlandson and Lyons, 1995).

Should the Concept of the Expendability of the Head's Time Be Acceptable?

Heads have rated activities in terms of their being most important and requiring most time. What is also of interest is that some of these activities were simultaneously identified as also being 'least important' and requiring 'most time' (Jirasinghe and Lyons 1995). What is being raised are issues relating to the position and role of the headteacher in schools in England and Wales. So often it seems that it is the head who has to pick up activities often of a supervisory, checking, clerical nature because no one else is available – driving the school minibus, refereeing a football match, waiting for and checking an important delivery serve as examples – disrupting perhaps more important ongoing activity. Similarly there are activities which are most important and upon which least time is spent. These would particularly include for this sample those activities that are classified under the learning/researching dimension.

The Issues of Size of School

In general the primary school is smaller than the secondary school (although it is recognized that primary schools can be larger than some secondary schools). The primary school has fewer resources; there is less scope for diversification of responsibility amongst staff, and its head also invariably functions as teacher and general factotum. However the range of tasks identified by primary and secondary heads are virtually identical; responsibilities and accountabilities while at times varying in magnitude are nevertheless held in common. It could well be a job as presently conceived, first, where the responsibilities and accountabilities placed upon the head of the small school are verging on the unviable and undeliverable. This point is also drawn attention to by Cooper and Kelly (1993) when reporting research concerning occupational stress amongst headteachers. Second, many primary schools, particularly in inner-city areas, are bigger than many secondary schools. Nevertheless the resourcing discrepancies between primary and secondary sectors remain and the scope for diversification of responsibility within its staff is correspondingly less.

If we turn specifically to those research results provided by the OPQ then other problem areas are identified.

Gender Issues and Stereotyping of Behaviours

The earlier section on the Occupational Personality Questionnaire identified that heads, when compared against the norm for managers and professional workers, tended to be for example, somewhat stronger on 'relationships to people', are less 'traditional', and more 'change orientated' etc. However differences within the headteachers group identified that male and female heads varied according to (some) behaviour and leadership style preferences. It is not clear however whether the differences observed were due to:

• genuine differences between male and female heads in preferred behaviours, for example in working with other people; or
• as a consequence of the need to conform to the differential expectations of appropriate behaviour for men and women held by those others surrounding the head (see for example Johnston 1986).

Indeed if the role a head plays is dependent upon the expectations of those around him or her, it may be the case that a female head modelling her behaviour upon her male equivalents (or vice versa) behaves in a way that is at odds with the expectations of her immediate audience. Thus in certain circumstances, a female head displaying such incongruous behaviour may be perceived by her audience as ineffectual in discharging her duties as head.

A large body of literature of effective management practice in general (e.g. Handy 1981; Peters and Waterman 1982; Adair 1988, 1990) and school management specifically (e.g. Caldwell and Spinks 1988; Everard 1988; Fullan 1991; Jenkins 1991) has emphasized the need to empower staff and work in teams and partnerships; to engage in consultations at all levels of the school's hierarchy; to be flexible and responsive; and to partake in collective decision making.

Gender differences between headteachers reported in the present research would seem to indicate that female heads would be more inclined than their male counterparts to engage in such participatory and consultative behaviour. Some theorists such as Shakeshaft (1993) have suggested that a 'feminine' management style is more appropriate to the needs of organizations, including schools, at the present time. However, males in our sample claim to be more 'data rational' than do their female colleagues an issue in a managerial world increasingly IT and quantitative data-orientated. It is not that females cannot undertake this aspect of their work, rather it is a personal inclination which raises questions for further exploration of job-person match or mismatch, and similarly for males regarding the managing people side of their work.

Therefore does the adoption of a more 'masculine' or 'feminine' management style serve as a constraint in the ability of the head to provide effective leadership to his or her school? It is clear that much further research is necessary before such claims can be seriously contemplated. Indeed it is likely that the style most appropriate to the effective running of our schools is one in which there is a balance of both 'masculine' and 'feminine' headteacher attributes.

However this proposition arises in a situation where clear incontrovertible evidence has not to date been put forward which establishes through an independent variable that one leadership style leads to more effective organizations; in fact it is unlikely that this would be the case. In these circumstances trainers will need to resolve how they would handle issues relating to 'delegative' styles of leadership, a preferred style identified by males in our sample, and to those heads whose preferred leadership styles are those of 'directive' and 'negotiative leadership'.

Such gender differences appear to be of immediate consequence and importance to the training, development, and selection and recruitment of headteachers. Each must address a number of significant issues, for example:

Training and development

Are differential approaches required to encompass the variations in preferred behaviour and leadership style shown by male and female headteachers?

Is the focus to be development of a balance of qualities stereotypically representing both male and female aspects or is one style or gender perspective to have pre-eminence over the other, or are all styles acceptable?

Selection and recruitment

At present prospective female candidates for headship probably seek to meet selection criteria which are predominantly 'male-orientated'. The significant skewed differences related to gender found in appointments to headships, for example in the secondary schools sector would seem to provide some underpinning for this claim (Edwards and Lyons 1994). If this assumption indeed proves to be the case a number of problems arise. First, women claim to have a preference to display distinctive behaviours and adopt a leadership style dissimilar to that of their male colleagues. Second, adoption by a female head of a management and leadership style which is essentially associated with her male equivalents may have repercussions for the effectiveness with which she is perceived to perform the job, since it is always likely to be unclear whether or not some or all others would expect her to behave in different ways to a male head.

Accountabilities

While heads in the sample overall indicated their preference for leadership which favours 'participatory' and 'consultative' styles, the context set by statute identifying the accountabilities of heads and/or governors can bring considerable strain into management predicated solely on these approaches. After all, they are the ones accountable for what occurs.

Caveats to the Head's Managerial Behaviours

Charles Handy (1981) has reminded us of some of the fundamental dilemmas for the manager which are always likely to be present:

- the manager should be culturally diverse and culturally flexible;
- management of the future goes hand in hand with management of the present;
- the manager must always balance trust against control;
- the manager must always seek to keep a proper balance between the needs of an individual, the demands of a group, and the demands of the total organization.

It appears from the research findings above that many complex behaviours have similarly and necessarily to be discharged by heads and that these may at times apparently appear as totally contradictory. Accordingly we would hypothesize a number of other caveats to the head's managerial behaviours. For example, heads claim their preferred ways of working to be *strongly democratic and strongly controlling*, that is on the one hand to encourage others to contribute, to consult, listen and refer to others, and on the other hand, to take charge, direct and supervise others.

The head would appropriately need to be *affiliative and not affiliative*, ensuring that they work effectively with people and groups, but that this does not lead to an excessive need to refer to others, or to seek interpersonal contact when it is inappropriate. Headteachers must also be *caring and not caring* ensuring they can give to and help those in need while appropriately being tough minded, deal with personal confrontation and balance this against a consciousness of the needs of all in their community.

Heads need to be both *change orientated and not change orientated*, and *traditional and not traditional*, ensuring that a balance can be provided between seizing on the new opportunity while not abandoning a well-proven way of working before it is demonstrably superseded, and avoiding the 'change for change's sake' syndrome. Additionally a head should display characteristics of being *relaxed and not relaxed*, and *worrying and not worrying*, ensuring that they can relax and leave the problems of the school behind, but that they must at times react with sufficient urgency and concern, certainly in meeting deadlines, not accept defeat too willingly, and use their anxiety to lift them for important occasions.

The head needs to be *critical and not critical* ensuring that they do not necessarily accept what is offered at face value and probe for the reasons behind decisions, proposals, actions, etc. and that they should do so while not appearing counterproductively negative or indecisive.

Finally, the head needs to *have emotional control and not have emotional control*; that is, while appearing calm and in control, a headteacher must remember to project warmth or enthusiasm.

It is unlikely that we would ever find a headteacher who fully met all of the criteria identified. Any head imports into the job his or her personal experience, skills, traits, attributes, motives, and self-concept, and as such there would immediately be a chemistry produced between head, school, and all of its stakeholders. There is a danger that the specification sought would need an Archangel Gabriel to fulfil all of its requirements. However, judgment and the selection of appropriate behaviours are obviously key aspects of effective headteacher performance.

The notion of an ideal head and how individuals match up to the demands of the ideal raises the argument about producing such 'perfect' specifications for use in an imperfect world. On the one hand we need these 'perfect' models to provide some kind of goal to aspire to, but on the other hand recognize that the goal is always beyond our reach. It is in this sense that compensatory behaviour and strategies become important. They are what give us hope that the goals we set ourselves may be achievable, and achievable in ways we might find satisfying. We carry these issues through into the next chapter concerning management competencies.

Note

1   STEN is an abbreviation for 'standard ten', a standard score system with a mean of 5.5 and a standard deviation of 2.

Part III

Practical Outcomes

Part III focuses on the practical outcomes from the research analysis and findings. One of the major outcomes to the research is the derivation of a set of management competencies for headteachers.

Competencies are primarily to do with assessment and diagnosis, that is, they underpin the assessment process. In so doing competencies have the capacity to greatly improve procedures for the recruitment and selection, management development and training, and appraisal of headteachers; first, by enhancing the effectiveness of each of these procedures through an approach to assessment which is more accurate, objective and standardized; second, by the use of the competence-based approach to demonstrate the fairness and impartiality of the procedures in addressing important issues regarding equal opportunities.

The competencies provide a framework by which a head may undertake an analysis of his or her managerial skills, identifying areas of strength and areas where development may be necessary. In this way heads may use the competencies to diagnose training needs, and to plan their own career progression.

Competence-based frameworks however must in the wider context be seen as part of an overall human resource strategy for a school which integrates individual (management) development with career development (encompassing the individual's motivation and aspirations) and with school development.

To be functionally useful for heads and schools, the competencies identified must be shown to be valid, and in the long term this will entail a demonstration of their use in predicting successful job performance. Thus the relationship between the competencies and headteacher and school effectiveness are issues towards which careful and deliberate steps must be taken.

Part III of the book considers such underlying issues and offers the first practical outcomes of the research by presenting in Chapter 4, the competency model for headteachers identified from the research, and in Chapter 5, discussing functional uses of the competence approach and the potential benefits to be derived for assessing and developing heads.

Chapter 4

A Competency Model of Headteachers

Introduction

A principal reason for the job analysis conducted in the research was to elicit information on headteachers for the purposes of identifying management competencies. The data produced by the Work Profiling System and the Occupational Personality Questionnaires were presented in Chapter 3. The competencies generated provide the basis of assessment criteria informing headteacher management development, recruitment and selection, appraisal and training, as well as head's personal and career development.

This chapter contains the identification of competencies for headteachers based upon the job analysis information collected in this research. The process of arriving at a 'competency model' for headteachers is described. Included is a discussion on establishing the validity of the competencies identified. This is vital to authentication of the competencies, ensuring their relevance, and indicating steps towards ascertaining their predictive value concerning job performance.

The headteacher management competencies derived from the present research are compared to other models in use with headteachers, and also with 'generic' models designed for use with all managers. With this comparison key general issues relating to competency approaches and their use are presented. Finally some issues are discussed as they apply to the uses of a competency model with headteachers. In this regard concerns centre upon the predictive validity of the competencies, particularly as competencies relate to headteacher performance and school effectiveness.

First the process of identifying the headteacher management competencies from the results of the job analysis is described. The main elements are outlined below. A more detailed description of the process can be found in Jirasinghe (1994).

Deriving a Set of Management Competencies for Headteachers

A two-stage approach to competency derivation was followed where the competencies are identified through an inferential process which builds on the outcomes to the job analysis. First, the job analysis phase details the tasks, responsibilities and behaviour requirements in the head's job. Second, the competency stage identifies the underlying characteristics/attributes.

Several instruments and techniques were employed in the initial job analysis phase; the Work Profiling System and Occupational Personality Questionnaire have already been described. Additionally, one-to-one interviews in the form of critical incidents with headteachers, and repertory grids with inspectors/advisers were conducted (see Chapter 1 for brief descriptions of these techniques). The interviews produced a list of those headteacher characteristics, abilities, skills and behaviours, seen by heads and inspectors/advisers, to differentiate successful from less successful job performance. Critical incidents and a repertory grid analysis proved to be a valuable source of job analysis material, adding depth and colour to the information collected through other methods. A brief synopsis and a summary of the data gathered through critical incidents and the repertory grids is presented in Appendix 4.

One of the major findings of the research is that some differences exist between heads working in different school sectors, yet there is an overwhelming similarity in the tasks and responsibilities of headteachers of primary and secondary schools (see Chapter 3). Thus the competencies derived in this research are generic in nature, applicable to heads working in a variety of contexts, including all the major school sectors.

The derived set of competencies may be viewed as a reference point encapsulating the competencies most heads would display most of the time. This is not to say that certain heads working in unusual settings and circumstances will not display some departure from the generic competencies. Indeed all heads may exhibit some competencies which are 'organization (school) specific' and 'individual specific'. Exclusions, additions and priority weighting to the generic set of competencies according to personal or school contextual factors may be useful. It is understood that local contexts produce differences in emphasis, prioritization, or urgency of competencies utilized rather than altering the list of competencies *per se*.

Mapping Tasks and Attributes into Competencies

Initial work in deriving the competencies took place at a Competence Workshop, a two-day event involving all job analysts, and a number of experienced professionals in the field of education management. The workshop comprised four stages:

1 *Sharing of all job analysis data* – The results from all aspects of the job analysis, in the form of tasks, attributes, skills etc., were gathered together and disseminated to all team members.
2 *Categorizations by individual members of the group* – At this stage each analyst individually sorts and categorizes tasks, abilities etc. to arrive at their own 'clusters' or 'competencies'. The contributions of different team members were then compared, similarities and differences identified, and followed by a discussion as to the most optimal clustering of the data. In general there was a large degree of agreement and overlap as to the most essential elements for the set of competencies to be derived from the data.
3 *Clustering of the job analysis information* – A consensus was reached as

to the clustering of tasks, skills, abilities etc. under appropriate headings, and the destination of *all* data (excluding repetitious items) agreed. These then formed the basic components of the competency.

4 *Drafting the competencies* – The first drafts of the competencies, encapsulating all tasks, skills, abilities etc. listed under each particular competency cluster heading, were produced by the workshop members. The competencies were regarded at this stage as 'working' competencies since they would undergo subsequent revision and alteration. It was important at this stage that workshop members agreed that the competencies identified:

- are distinct and separate from each other with no overlap or duplication; and
- faithfully represent the findings of the job analysis conducted, i.e. no aspect of the data derived from the job analysis process is left unaccounted for.

The Format of the Competencies

Having arrived at the essential components to each competency, two pilots of the competencies, first with headteachers and second with inspectors/advisers, provided further revision and fine tuning of the competencies. For example, the competencies required a clear structure; they needed to be readily packaged and user-friendly. Each competency was shaped to follow a standard format of 'personal transferable competencies' for use in many contexts. That is, each competency comprises:

- a title;
- a short summary definition encapsulating the competency; and
- a set of key assessable/observable 'behavioural indicators' which enables the competency to be assessed.

Behavioural indicators must provide unambiguous statements of successful performance of each competency. They serve as the interface between the definition of a competency in an abstract sense, and its assessment, and as such are a key part of competence specification.

For ease of use a restricted set of competencies is necessary, perhaps between 10 to 15, grouped under four or five overarching 'competence areas'. The headteacher competencies derived here totalled 14 discrete competencies. In providing a 'map' of the characterization of a head's job offered by the competencies, the competencies were clustered into five overarching areas or groupings (see below). In a practical sense, competencies are artefacts assembled from a finite list of tasks, skills, attributes etc. relating to the job at a particular point in time.

It is apparent that competency identification is an open system such that:

- all possible competencies will never be completely defined or identified;
- some competencies identified will not have any distinctive means of assessment or attainment; and
- some competencies will be simple and mundane while others will appear to be complex and abstract.

Validating the Headteacher Competencies

In specifying competence it is necessary that each competency:

- is assessable and can be used constructively by the field;
- reflects an aspect of the head's job;
- is independent of the other competencies;
- has meaning and relevance to the field; and
- that it is correlated with personal and organizational job performance.

All of the above criteria pertain to differential aspects of the 'validity' of the competencies. Validity characterizing whether or not the competencies measure what they were designed to measure embraces a variety of forms. At a minimal level the requirements of 'face' and 'content' validity must be satisfied.

- *Face validity* measuring whether the competencies are seen as acceptable and relevant by all those in a particular occupational area, has been established for the headteacher competencies, a process described below.
- *Content validity* assesses the extent to which the set of identified competencies samples the behavioural domain of the job under study, i.e. do the headteacher competencies relate to the actual job activities of a head? Content validity rests on the job analysis conducted. The job analysis undertaken for the headteacher position through its comprehensive and detailed nature, and involving a large sample of heads, has ensured the content validity of the headteacher competencies.
- *'Construct' validity*, which assesses the degree to which the competencies measure the traits and 'constructs' which actually underlie job performance and to which the competencies refer, is more difficult to achieve.
- *Criterion validity*, determining the relationship between a head's competency assessment and his or her job performance, is subdivided into:

  concurrent validity, measuring the correlation between an individual head's competency assessment and some criterion of job performance obtained *at the same time*; and
  predictive validity, the extent to which the head's competency assessment is a predictor of job performance sometime *in the future*.

An empirical validation of the headteacher management competencies as represented by concurrent/predictive validity is in the long term a necessary activity.

The particular problems posed for the education sector in attempting to meet these criteria are discussed towards the end of this chapter. Needless to say content and face validity may be more immediately and practically realizable in the schools sector. The establishment of the face validity of the headteacher competencies is described next.

Establishing the Face Validity of the Headteacher Management Competencies

In order that the competencies generated are of maximum use to those in the school sector, it has been necessary to establish with heads, as well as deputy heads and inspectors/advisers, the accuracy, relevance and appropriateness of the identified competencies. That is, it must be verified with heads that the language used is acceptable, and that the competencies are appropriate for heads in all school sectors and working under different contexts at the current time. Also it must be ensured that the implicit model of management contained within the competencies is not unfairly biased toward any specific group, for example towards a traditionally masculine model of management.

In addition to the small group pilot work conducted with heads and inspectors/advisers, a large scale survey of 100 headteachers was conducted. Heads comprised a subsample of the original research sample, chosen at random, but constructed to represent all the major headteacher and school variables, and the population of heads across England and Wales. This work was additionally supplemented with some small group work with deputy heads and inspectors/advisers (see Jirasinghe 1994 for more detailed information). It was also necessary to solicit the perceptions of significant others, for example additional schools staff, parents, and governors etc., as to the appropriateness of the competencies identified.

The research survey conducted with headteachers was in the form of a postal questionnaire. The questionnaire presented heads with the competencies and asked whether the competencies could be reasonably applied to all heads in all sectors, and whether they were sufficiently intelligible as they stood or required improvements in drafting, clarity etc.

Additionally, the appropriateness of the 'competence areas', and the identification of any key competencies heads felt had been omitted was sought. Heads were also asked to provide a number of actual work incidents which might illustrate positive performance on each competency. The latter, it was hoped, would provide a useful check for the accuracy of behavioural indicators specified.

Analysis of returns revealed a great deal of agreement amongst headteachers. For example, heads were almost unanimous in their conviction that the full complement of competencies specified would be as important for an infant/first, junior and primary head, as for a secondary head.

A large number of specific work-based indicators were supplied by heads for each competency identified, perhaps giving an indication of the current breadth and range of the head's work. The former provided corroboratory evidence as to the distinctness and relevance of the behavioural indicators, and the information was used to ensure that the behavioural indicators would be 'assessable'.

Headteachers also agreed that the competencies were generally sufficiently intelligible as presented and the overarching 'competence areas' suitable and relevant. No significant new competencies were suggested as possible omissions, but several heads alluded to an 'added ingredient' such as 'charisma' or 'flair'. Interestingly these heads felt that this extra component made a significant contribution to effectiveness but it defied simple definition and explanation, and could probably not be sufficiently captured in a competence model for headteachers.

It is also worth mentioning here that several heads expressed the (personal) developmental benefits of questionnaire completion; the process of thinking about their job as head proved an exacting, yet extremely positive experience.

The Headteacher Management Competencies

Subsequent to the completion of any amendments resulting from the face validation survey, the outcome to the process was a set of competencies for headteachers, piloted and validated with heads, as well as a smaller number of deputy heads and inspectors/advisers. The finalized set of competencies is presented in Table 4.1 and discussed below. It reflects all the major current dimensions of headship, applicable to the main school sectors.

Table 4.1: The headteacher management competencies

Competence areas	Competencies
The planning and administrative process	Analyzing Planning Directional leadership
Dealing with people	Sensitivity Motivating Evaluating
Managing the political environment	Political ability Persuading and negotiating
Professional and technical knowledge	Professional knowledge Technical knowledge
Personal skills	Commitment and values Reasoning and judgment Self-awareness and development Projecting a favourable image and communicating

The Planning and Administrative Process

Analyzing

Is able to analyze contextual factors, diagnose difficulties and seek necessary information in order to inform vision, generate and evaluate alternatives for action and to provide the basis for future planning.

Planning

Uses vision and a future orientation to develop long term goals and strategies, as well as planning to meet immediate problems and needs. Initiates and develops planning procedures for curriculum, community, staff, pupils and budgetary matters.

Directional leadership

Sets standards and gives direction to the school. Makes decisions, and devises and implements administrative systems for organizing human and other resources. Brings tasks successfully to completion by delegation and through appropriate use of time and attention to detail.

Dealing with People

Sensitivity

Is accessible, sensitive, and uses tact and diplomacy in helping pupils, parents, staff and governors.

Motivating

Motivates and mobilizes others by promoting an ethos of excellence, individual and team development, and collaborative decision making. Provides support and resources to maximize personal and professional development.

Evaluating

Promotes confidence amongst staff and pupils by setting up systems to enable monitoring and evaluating of their work and progress. Appraises staff strengths and needs for purposes of personal development and recruitment, retention and promotion.

Managing the Political Environment

Political ability

Is politically adept, can develop and maintain a network of contacts, and is aware of own relationship to the wider political environment. Generates support amongst stakeholders for the school.

Persuading and negotiating

Is persuasive and negotiates with various interest groups, if necessary being tough minded and firm in dealing with conflicts in order to achieve a successful outcome.

The Competent Head

Professional and Technical Knowledge

Professional knowledge

Exercises knowledge of matters appertaining to the management of the curricular, instructional, pedagogic and welfare processes to give firm educational leadership to the school and community.

Technical knowledge

Has knowledge of, and can deal efficiently with, the legal, statutory, financial and budgetary processes currently impinging upon the school.

Personal Skills

Commitment and values

Displays commitment to the school through strength of personal beliefs, by own energy and enthusiasm and by maintaining own morale.

Reasoning and judgment

Is able to reason logically with verbal, written and numerical data, critically evaluate information received, and exercise judgment in making decisions and solving problems.

Self-awareness and development

In recognizing the need for continuous personal and professional development, keeps abreast of new educational developments, actively monitors own performance and has wider interests outside the school. Is able to respond to change by generating ideas for organizational renewal.

Projecting a favourable image and communicating

Establishes visibility and credibility for school by confidently projecting the school and its goals. Communicates effectively both orally and in writing, even when under pressure, adapting style according to the audience.

It is worth reiterating here that many coalitions of competencies are conceivable to form 'competence areas', and there is potentially an almost limitless clustering and assemblage of behaviours, skills and attributes upon which competencies could be formed. In this context it is recognized that the competence area of 'personal skills' for example could potentially have encompassed other competencies, for example, the competencies of sensitivity, and persuading and negotiating. It is our contention that the presentation above represents an accurate and useful picture of the job of headteacher. Continued testing can add to data concerning relevance to the field, and the uses to which the competencies can be put.

Comparisons with Other Competence Models Developed for Headteachers and Managers

Applications of competence models to headteachers are few. The tendency has been not to apply models which have been specifically developed and validated in the UK, which are based on a rigorous research base, or which are based upon a large sample of headteachers. The present research has attempted to rectify the above shortcomings.

A comparison of our headteacher management competencies with those produced by others serves two main purposes. The first purpose is to point the reader towards other competence models employed with heads (Esp 1993 has provided one succinct account of these) and the second is to identify commonalities and differences between the various approaches.

A framework was developed earlier (see Figure 2.7) which enabled us to view competencies as consisting of those which are generic across the majority of senior managerial positions, those competencies which are specific to and define a particular occupational sector/area, and those competencies that are uniquely individual and organizational (school) based.

A comparison of headteacher competence models with competence frameworks designed for managers in general may highlight those competencies that appear to be generic to the act of management. This comparison may also identify those competencies that seem to be specific to education management and headteachers.

The following represents a selective review of (published) competency approaches to school and 'generic' management, currently in use in the UK. A brief description is presented of each competence approach; the competencies from each are displayed in Appendix 5. The selected approaches are:

- *London Borough of Kensington and Chelsea*: Kensington and Chelsea commissioned Hay/McBer Management Consultants to define those qualities required by headteachers in order to provide effective management to their schools. Hay/McBer identified 18 competencies, arranged into five overarching clusters (see London Borough of Kensington and Chelsea/Hay Management Consultants 1990).
- *The National Association of Secondary School Principals* (NASSP), with the help of the American Psychological Association first introduced the assessment centre process to school principals in the USA some 20 years ago. The NASSP model, validated with 42 high school principals in 1981 (Schmitt *et al.* 1981), has 12 identified 'skill dimensions'.
- *The National Educational Assessment Centre*, originally set up by the Secondary Heads Association and Oxford Polytechnic (now Oxford Brooks

University) with some further support from government and industry, has introduced the NASSP competencies into the UK with some emendation for senior school managers in the UK (see NEAC 1995).

- *School Management South (SMS)/Employment Department*: School Management South, a regional consortium of 14 LEAs in the southeast of England, has used the framework and methodology advocated by the Employment Department and the NCVQ, i.e. functional analysis, to produce a set of occupational standards for school management (Earley 1992; 1993).
- *Teacher Training Agency 'Headlamp' Initiative*: Headlamp, a national scheme falling under the aegis of the Teacher Training Agency (TTA) is designed to support newly-appointed headteachers. The TTA has developed a set of six 'leadership and management *tasks*' and a range of eight 'leadership and management *abilities*' required of headteachers (see TTA 1995).

Clusters of *generic* competencies which are widely used include Saville and Holdsworth's Inventory of Management Competencies, those for senior managers still being piloted by the Management Charter Initiative and also those originally produced by Richard Boyatzis in the 1980s as The McBer/Boyatzis competencies. There are of course many other lists of competencies produced by individual organizations, who, invariably starting from a generic listing, fine-tune its 'original' competencies to the needs of their particular occupation sector and the particular job which is focused upon.

An analysis of these various sets of competencies indicates at least five broad issues. First of all, allowing for different use of language and labelling, a number of similarities are shown across the models of managerial competence for both headteachers and 'managers in general'. For example the competencies of analyzing, planning, directional leadership, sensitivity, motivating, commitment and values (usually in the form of drive/commitment rather than values for the managers), reasoning and judgment, self-awareness and development, and projecting a favourable image and communicating (see Appendix 5) seem to be common to the two groups.

There are a substantial number of competencies that are generic and which all managers would claim are necessary towards effective performance of their jobs. This is not to say that planning as undertaken by a headteacher for a school is the same as planning by a manager of a commercial organization, or even that of a public sector manager in the health service. While the generic process of planning may be similar, the actual content and nature of the activity may be very different. This variance should be reflected in the behavioural indicators specified under each competency. Behavioural indicators therefore contextualize each competency.

Another issue arises here, that of the 'level' at which the competency is to be performed. McCleary (1973) has divided competence into three performance levels: familiarity, understanding, and application. Thus a competency may be judged to be required for a particular position, for example for an infant head at an application level, at an understanding level for a secondary head, and yet another level such as familiarity for a non-educational sector manager. The specification of competency levels therefore presents a useful way of examining the interfacing of competencies for various roles, and can also be used in preparing headteachers to move from one role to another.

Also, particular areas within an occupation and between occupations are valued differently. McCleary (1984) has described a 'social-value environment' which applies criteria for competence differently across domains, for example, the variance in rigour used to describe 'judgment' by a physician and a teacher. Thus while both headteachers and non-education sector managers may show commonalities in terms of competencies, there are likely to be differences pertaining to how some competencies are valued across occupational domains, or indeed even across the various school sectors.

Second, a number of competencies distinguish the headteacher competence models as compared to those for managers, for example, in the area of managing the political environment, the competencies of 'political ability' and 'persuading and negotiating'. Also the competence of 'evaluating' relating to monitoring and evaluating staff progress and dealing with selection, retention, promotion etc. tends to be omitted from generic management lists. The latter may be as a result of the head carrying responsibility for functions which in most other organizations would be handed over to a separate personnel section. Additionally the headteacher competence models tend to place a greater emphasis on the place of 'values' and specific expertise in underpinning job performance (see Appendix 5).

Competencies which seem to be particularly pertinent to and distinguish headteachers may not however be static. They may be affected by change and fluctuation in the nature of the job according to the prevalent political and social environment in which the head works. For example, competencies which are associated with a period of change such as 'living with uncertainty' and 'coping with conflict' may be transitional, i.e. relevant for only a short period of time.

Third, there is some variation in the headteacher competence models depicted in Appendix 5. Some models offer a greater coverage than others of the skills and attributes revealed as important in the present research for headteachers. In particular most of the 'other' headteacher competence models cited above seemed to neglect the political dimension to the head's role except for the mention of the need to form networks. The competency relating to persuading and convincing others provides another case in point. Similarly, there is little coverage of the professional and technical knowledge underpinning job performance.

Fourth, the number of competencies in each of the models cited above varies greatly, from 12 in the National Association of Secondary School Principals (NASSP) model to 41 elements, each of these with its own set of performance criteria, in the School Management South (SMS) or 36 elements for management II of the Management Charter Initiative Standards. The more 'factors' or competencies in the model therefore the greater is the likelihood of coverage in all important job areas. There is however an exponential relationship with flexibility and ease of use; the larger the list the more unwieldy and cumbersome and the more restricted its use. A list like that produced by the MCI or SMS may be suitable for appraisal or the identification of specific training needs, but is not likely to be appropriate for a selection and recruitment exercise, or the identification of management potential. For the latter it is necessary to have an efficient list of competencies that provides maximum coverage for the lowest number of competencies possible. Adoption of a particular competence model needs to be based upon purpose and usage.

Finally, the headteacher management competencies developed as a result of the present research comprise the main elements which seem common to management, but also those competencies which seem to differentiate the work of headteachers at the current time. Competencies predicated by individual headteachers, and/or school circumstances, cannot appear in such a generic list of competencies. The latter will need to be locally determined and appended to the identified list, or the existing competencies modified accordingly.

Thus far in this chapter we have described the process of generating management competencies and establishing the face validity of the competencies. We have also looked at a number of other competence models and highlighted a number of broad issues. All competence models described however must have the capacity to distinguish effective from less effective job performance, and to predict either current or future job performance. The following sections therefore discuss issues as regards the 'predictive validity' of the headteacher competencies, and the relationship of the competencies to headteacher and school effectiveness.

Towards Predictive Validity

It is necessary that the competencies identified have the capacity to differentiate between headteachers or between candidates for headship. In the long term it is imperative that the headteacher competencies are shown to be related to either effective current (concurrent validity) or future (predictive validity) job performance. The present research has focused on content and face validity. However the basis for a more empirical validation of the competencies has been established.

The identification of competencies for heads has led to the development of an assessment centre for headteachers at the East London Business School, University of East London (assessment centres are described in greater detail in the following chapter) where the headteacher management competencies together with their behavioural indicators constitute the assessment criteria. It was suggested earlier that the assessment centre process represents the best available technique for assessing an individual's competence (see Chapter 2).

The ability of the assessment centre process, underpinned by the competencies, to accurately produce a differentiation between heads, correlating with an independent measure of job performance, represents one approach to establishing the concurrent validity of the competencies. An independent measure of 'effectiveness' may, for example, be secured through a process of superordinate and peer nomination. In this way the first steps may be taken towards establishing the predictive validity of the headteacher competencies.

An incremental approach is necessary in establishing confidence in the competence model derived for headteachers. As a first step, face and content validity have been satisfied. Faith and confidence in the first steps enables us to advance on to the next phase, which is the concurrent validity of the competencies. This, in turn, permits progression to the next stage of predictive validity, and so on. In this way, we are able to take steps towards a competence model for headteachers that is related to personal, and ultimately also to organizational, performance.

The Relationship of Competence to Headteacher and School Effectiveness

A specification of competence carries the implicit assumption that the skills and qualities contained within the competence model are associated with effective headteacher behaviour. Thus the competencies represent a framework describing the essential elements for effective headship. The emphasis here is on 'effectiveness' at the personal level and moves away from the tendency to measure headteacher effectiveness on the basis of direct organizational performance or school effectiveness.

In describing an effective headteacher, however, are we also describing an effective school? Work by influential writers on the topic of school effectiveness (e.g. Caldwell and Spinks 1988; Fullan 1991) has linked successful leadership by school leaders to the establishment of an effective school. For example, Caldwell, arguing for the 'self-managing' school (Caldwell and Spinks 1988; Caldwell 1994), has emphasized the role of the principal as leader and manager as being very important to the success of the school. The leadership should be in the form of appropriate consultation with stakeholders, with goal setting, planning, and decision making carried out in teams at the management level and among staff in their areas of interest and expertise.

There are however a number of major obstacles in ascertaining the relationship between a head's management behaviour and the effectiveness of his or her school. One of the major problems lies in securing agreed measures of school effectiveness. Nationally applicable criteria, which have been imposed by government in the UK, to date have included Standard Achievement Tests for Schools (SATS), public examination results, pupil attendance, delinquency rates, staff turnover etc. but these measures are criticized for failing to take sufficient note of 'value added'. For example, a school serving a very deprived community judged against national norms may appear to be performing badly. However, this may fail to take account first, of improvements that have been made over the last one or two years, and second, the extent of their impact on pupils and the local community where that school's performance is now viewed very positively.

It is also difficult to infer what relationship, causal or otherwise, might exist between factors which are thought to contribute to school success and school effectiveness itself. Therefore a second problem lies in disentangling cause from effects. For example, is it the competent head who creates the effective school or the effective school which manifests the competent head?

It is likely that the specification of headteacher competence will lead to an effectively managed school with successful outcomes, but it is by no means a *fait accompli*. Numerous issues, for example the nature of the intake, the competence and ability of staff, context/environment factors, may intervene between the actions of a head and any measure of school effectiveness. The issue here is the isolation of the 'independent variable'.

As before it is necessary to proceed by way of incremental stages. The first step in verifying the predictive validity of the competencies has been described above, that is, establishing that a competent head will be a successful job performer. In progressing to the next stage, we can be fairly confident (for example from much previous research) that the effectiveness of the head is likely to contribute to the success of the school. Further research is however necessary to ascertain the exact nature of the interaction between these two reciprocal elements. The competency assessment process provides a means to do this.

No claims are made to resolve substantial problems that have so troubled the schools sector and, recognizing that further research is necessary to determine the exact nature of these relationships, it is suggested that an approach as presented here will lay the basis for a demonstration that it is a competent head, who is an effective head and who runs a successful school.

Summary and Conclusions

The results from all aspects of the job analysis was used to derive management competencies for headteachers. The initial work was conducted at a competence workshop, and supplemented by a succession of piloting workshops with heads and inspectors/advisers. The derived competencies followed a standard format, with sets of key behavioural indicators, enabling each competency to be assessed. The competencies, numbering 14 in all, and clustered into five overarching competence areas, are also generic in nature, applicable to a variety of heads working in different contexts, including the major school sectors.

In establishing the validity of the identified competencies content validity has been assumed through the rigour and comprehensive nature of the job analysis conducted on heads. The face validity of the competencies has been demonstrated through workshops and further field work involving a questionnaire survey of 100 headteachers.

The headteacher management competencies derived from the present research have been compared to a number of other headteacher competence models in use, as well as to some 'generic' competence models applicable to a range of managers working in different occupational areas. This analysis has revealed that a number of competencies are common to both headteachers and managers in general. The generic processes underlying each of these competencies may be similar, however the actual content of the competencies as represented by the behavioural indicators will vary across occupational areas.

Further, a number of competencies would seem to delineate headteachers and distinguish them from other managers. The set of competencies derived in the present research would include elements that apply to managers in general but would also incorporate competencies that are representative of the occupation of headteacher.

Finally, in focusing solely on headteachers, there is some variation in the headteacher competence models depicted. Some approaches offer greater coverage than others of the headteacher skills and attributes revealed as important in the present research. The headteacher competencies derived from the research are presented as up-to-date and relevant and representing the essential features of the head's job. Selection of a model should be dependent not only on the extent of coverage of important areas, but also on the flexibility and efficiency of its use.

In the longer term, it is important that the identified competencies demonstrate predictive validity, that is, that they forecast future job performance. The use of performance measures in an assessment centre process underpinned by the headteacher management competencies, and its correlation with an independent measure of job performance, is identified as the first step towards this goal. An incremental approach has been adopted to establish confidence in the competence model derived for headteachers, in order to lay the basis for a demonstration of the validity of the competence model to effect both headteacher and school effectiveness.

Chapter 5

Assessing and Developing Headteachers

Introduction

The headteacher management competencies and competency-based assessment in general can be used in a number of significant ways to benefit headteachers and schools. Esp (1993) describes 30 or more ways to use a competence framework. To date, the major applications of competencies with heads have been for:

- selection and recruitment;
- management development and training;
- individual (self) development;
- team development; and
- headteacher appraisal.

While the focus here is on headteachers, it is however worth bearing in mind that many aspects of the discussion may be generalized to other staff in school as well.

This chapter considers some of the advantages to be derived from the adoption of a competence framework to the selection and recruitment, to the management development and training, and to the appraisal of headteachers. An example of a competency-based self-evaluation exercise is presented in Appendix 6.

Competency-Based Recruitment and Selection

A competency-based approach can contribute to selection and recruitment procedures in schools in two main ways. First, by improving the effectiveness of the selection and recruitment system, and second as a means of justifying the fairness of the system.

As regards selection and recruitment, the process of competency analysis takes into account the differential expectations of key members of school staff. It also recognizes the nature of staffs' current and changing (future) roles, and indicates the part that selection and recruitment plays in the development of an overarching human resource strategy for the school. Competency-based analysis, by clarifying roles and expectations, can expedite the development of a sense of school mission and cohesion, and the identification of a set of common objectives.

Once a competency analysis is complete the often haphazard nature of selection and recruitment decisions can be avoided (Feltham 1992). The competencies provide a 'visible set of agreed standards or criteria' for an approach to selection and recruitment that is objective and standardized. In this way greater confidence is engendered in selection procedures that are systematic in approach, and consistent across their use.

Best results may be obtained by the application of a competence framework in all stages of the recruitment process, including targeting and advertising, the application form, and pre-screening, as well as the selection of appropriate competency-led assessment methods. Conveying accurate information about the nature of the job through the 'language' of competencies (Feltham 1992) may be an important step, not only for the recruiting school but also for the prospective headteacher in making an informed choice as to personal suitability for the position under offer.

Competence-based selection methods are based on the hypothesis that the better the fit between the requirements of a job and competencies of the job holder, the higher the job performance and job satisfaction will be (Spencer and Spencer 1993). Successful job–person matching therefore requires

Table 5.1: Criterion validity correlations of commonly used assessment methods

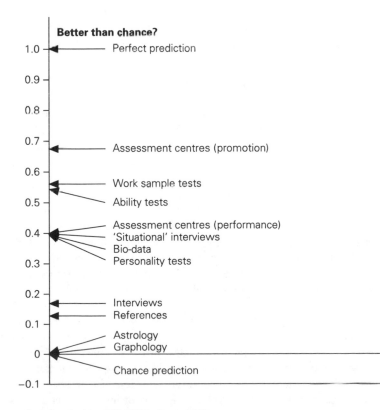

Source: Dr Mike Smith of UMIST in Rees 1989

- an accurate evaluation of an individual's competence;
- a reliable competency model of the job such as that presented here for headteachers;
- arriving at the 'goodness of fit' between an individual and the job.

Competence assessment may be achieved by a variety of means. A review of the most common assessment methods by Smith (see Rees 1989) has presented the criterion validity correlations of each method with job performance (see Table 5.1). The competence assessment method with the highest criterion validity correlation, the assessment centre process, is presented here as the most valid assessment technique currently available to assess headteachers. Further, evidence from 'utility analysis' on the cost-effectiveness of selection using the assessment centre has been well documented (Cascio and Silbey 1979; Hogan and Zenke 1986). The assessment centre process is described in greater detail below.

The above discussion indicated how the application of a competency-based approach can increase the **effectiveness** of selection procedures. A competency-based approach can additionally be used in **justifying** the selection and recruitment system. If assessment is built on clearly defined and measurable competencies derived from job analysis, then perceptual errors affecting assessors' judgments due to bias in gender, race, disability or age, are substantially reduced. The capacity of a competence-based approach to address issues of equal opportunities provides a compelling argument in favour of its use.

Competency-Based Management Development and Training

The headteacher management competencies enable an assessment to be made of a head identifying his or her strengths and development points. This 'profile' of the head then becomes the focus for his or her personal development through the diagnosis of development and training needs. The process may be replicated with deputy heads, identifying the potential for progression and areas of possible shortfall, thereby identifying areas for further training and development.

Thus competency-based assessment for management development purposes is essentially about the diagnostic process. Fletcher, S. (1991) has stated that misunderstandings about competence-based systems and about competence-based training usually arise from a mistaken belief that the former are systems of training rather than of assessment. Further, there is an erroneous conviction that the actual process or methods of designing training will radically change and that training will no longer be the remit of the trainer.

Competence-based approaches foster personal responsibility for, and control over, development and training. There may be a greater role for superordinates, a 'critical friend', or a mentor in facilitating the process. The role of the trainer (Fletcher S. 1991) becomes one of 'consultant' in identifying with headteachers and mentors heads' development needs, the design and delivery of training, and in evaluating the effectiveness of the provision. The role of mentoring is discussed in greater detail below.

The present circumstances under which schools operate predicates that head-teachers be more proactive and flexible in managing their personal and career development in the future. Correspondingly management development strategies need to evolve where they can function at the level of support to heads at the present time. Competencies may provide the best available approach in fulfilling these aims.

In this context it is crucial that the head's management development programme:

- be planned and coordinated;
- directly relates to the competency development needs identified as a result of the competence assessment;
- consists of an 'action plan' with measurable outputs;
- is designed to address issues pertinent to school development, i.e. the school development plan; and
- is conceived as part of an ongoing policy of improvement.

Prior to development work undertaken with headteachers, a more holistic, diagnostic process may be necessary. One that is capable of both an objective assessment of skills and abilities, as well as a more subjective personal view of a head's interests and motivation is particularly important in the education sector where personal development and individuality is highly valued.

Jacobs and Vyakarnam (1994) point out that an individual's level of skills and abilities derived from an assessment centre exercise does not reliably indicate how motivated that individual actually will be to utilize those abilities back at work. Motivational and career issues need to be considered and linked to the objective assessment of skill and competency development needs to form a complete picture of the head and his or her potential for success in school.

In this regard Jacobs (1989) suggests that there may be considerable value in 'peer group assessment' and the adoption of a '360 degree view' – self, superordinate, peer and subordinate perspectives – described in more detail later in the chapter.

Using Competencies to Support Headteacher Appraisal

The success of any appraisal system is dependent upon the extent to which it is viewed as providing an objective and fair assessment of an individual's work performance. Competencies are a means of underpinning, or at the very least of supporting, the formal appraisal procedures in schools. This is so because appraisal schemes tend to be constructed around irrelevant or dated criteria and because assessment scales are prone subjective biases.

Competencies facilitate the self-appraisal aspects of the headteacher appraisal cycle. The comparison of the head's self-evaluation with an independent assessment made by a 'significant other' also prepares heads for the appraisal discussion. The process of self-evaluation/self-assessment is discussed in further detail later in the chapter.

The adoption of a competence approach highlights differences and difficulties and provides a more honest review of performance. Further, the systematic and consistent approach to appraisal offered by a competence-based procedure is preferable to more *ad hoc* attempts to identify development and training needs.

A well designed and implemented appraisal will provide an accurate review of performance, and give heads the opportunity to consider, with the aid and support of a colleague(s), their own personal and professional development. Constraints on the head's time means that appraisal represents one of the rare occasions when such a dialogue can take place. For more information on appraisal the reader may wish to consult Fletcher (1993) or in focusing specifically on headteacher appraisal, Gane and Morgan (1992) or Fidler and Cooper (1992).

We have considered how the use of a competence-based approach can enhance the effectiveness of procedures for recruiting and selecting, training and developing, and appraising headteachers. The use of competencies to underpin these procedures is focused upon improving one key stage of each procedure, that of diagnosis and assessment. Our focus is competency-based assessment.

Several competence assessment techniques were briefly highlighted in Section 3 of Chapter 2. The remainder of this chapter discusses in greater depth some significant methods of competence assessment for use with heads in recruitment and selection, training, development and appraisal. These include:

- the use of the assessment centre process;
- self-evaluation using the headteacher management competencies;
- the 360 degree approach to assessing and developing headteachers; and
- the use of a mentoring partner.

The Assessment Centre Process

Assessment centres utilizing multiple assessors, and multiple assessment techniques such as in-trays, group exercises, presentations and role plays etc., are used in non-educational employment sectors for a variety of purposes (see Chapter 2, Section 3 for a description). Their use in education in the USA is now also widespread (McCleary and Ogawa 1989). Until recently however there were few attempts in the UK to apply the assessment centre concept systematically to education and the schools sector, the assessment centres for headteacher set up at the East London Business School (Lyons and Jirasinghe 1992), and at Oxford by NEAC/SHA (Oliver 1992) being the obvious exceptions.

Variety and Flexibility of Use

Assessment centres can be used in a variety of ways. For example they are commonly employed

- for recruitment and selection;
- for diagnosing individual training and development needs; and
- for career planning.

For the organization they can be used

- for assessing potential for promotion and in succession planning;
- to facilitate institutional planning; and
- to optimize the talent in the organization by keeping good people motivated.

Their use also

- presents job holders with a clear picture of the organization's commitment towards their development; and
- can serve as a useful 'public relations' exercise for the organization in displaying its professional approach to recruiting and developing its staff.

A centre is also likely to be a rich source of development for an organization in

- team building;
- developing skills necessary for future effectiveness; and
- in helping to bring about a cultural transformation.

The Advantages of Assessment Centres

Since assessment centres are built on representative 'samples' of materials and situations from the job-domain, content validity is inherent within the process. As regards predictive validity, many studies indicate a strong positive relationship between assessment centre ratings and future job performance (see for example, Rees 1989 – summarized in Table 5.1; also Schmitt *et al.* 1984 and Gaugler *et al.* 1987). By way of example, a study of promotion rates in the American Telephone and Telegraph company (Moses and Byham 1977) found that candidates who had been given assessment centre ratings of 'more than acceptable' were twice as likely to be promoted several times than individuals rated as 'acceptable'. Also, the former were nearly 10 times more likely to be promoted than individuals rated as 'not acceptable'.

As regards equal opportunities, most studies have shown that similar proportions of women to men have been identified, and that overall centre ratings and specific criterion ratings are equally predictive of subsequent managerial success for men and women (Dale and Iles 1992).

Huck and Bray (1976) compared black and white non-management women who attended an assessment centre during a five year period and who were later promoted. Of the assessors, 35 per cent were woman and a small proportion, 5 per cent, were black. They found no significant difference between white and black subjects in the correlations of overall assessment ratings with overall job performance or potential for advancement. The assessment centre method is therefore identified as especially attractive for affirmative action such as the accelerated advancement of minority groups and women. It must however be acknowledged that the assessment centre process as a whole needs to be inspected for potential bias including assessment centre nomination, prescreening procedures, assessment centre publicity etc. (Alban-Metcalfe 1989).

An additional advantage lies in the benefit to assessors of assessment centre training and participation. Serving as an assessor on an assessment centre can be a most beneficial developmental experience, often increasing motivation and improving assessors' own managerial skills (Lorenzo 1984; Bawtree and Hogg 1989).

Since the cost of errors in selection for senior managerial positions tends to be extremely high, the cost-effectiveness of the assessment centre approach, a measure of its so-called 'utility', is also claimed to be significant. Cascio and Silbey (1979) state that under most operational uses, assessment centres could be expected to provide a return on investment of at least 600 per cent and that it would not be unusual to achieve a return as high as 1000 per cent.

Hogan and Zenke (1986), evaluating four selection procedures for hiring school principals in the USA, found that selected assessment centre exercises had the greatest utility with an expected dollar-value performance gain in excess of $58,000 over the traditional interview alternative.

Difficulties with the Approach

In espousing the use of assessment centres as the most effective method presently available to measure and assess competence, it is wise to be aware of pitfalls confronting the assessment centre process. Drawbacks to the process may be surmounted through careful assessment centre design and operation.

Difficulties may arise with:

1 *Assessors and assessment centre dimensions or competencies*: Sackett and Hakel (1979) found that assessors used only a small number of dimensions in making their judgments. In fact, evidence suggests that too many dimensions can impair the ability of an assessor to cope effectively. Three dimensions (leadership, organizational planning, and decision making) accurately predicted overall ratings. There is also a tendency, by assessors, to rate performance on the exercise as a whole, rather than to evaluate performance on each single dimension or competency (Sackett and Hakel 1979). The above would seem to point in no uncertain terms to the crucial nature of thorough, rigorous, and continuous training for assessors.

2 *Construct validity*: Sackett and Dreher (1982) conclude that there is little evidence that assessment centre ratings measure the complex traits they purport to measure. It is also claimed that certain 'soft' qualities such as impact, creativity, sensitivity etc. are difficult to measure in assessment centres (Jacobs 1989).

3 *Predictive validity*: In using promotions or 'level achieved' as the criterion (i.e. the measure of job performance) many validity studies have suffered from 'criterion contamination'. That is, assessment centre ratings have

been used as part of promotion decisions, and therefore the observed correlation between centre ratings and management level achieved is artificially inflated (Blanksby and Iles 1990). However it is worth noting that some studies controlling for this eventuality have found evidence supporting the predictive validity of assessment centres (e.g. Bray 1982).

4 *Equal opportunities*: While one of the major advantages of the assessment centre process is its objective and non-discriminatory approach to assessment, one needs to be alert to a number of issues where bias can occur. For example:

- Black women's ratings have been adversely effected with an increase in the proportion of white male assessors (Schmitt and Hill 1977). Strict dictates and procedures may therefore have to be adopted in selecting managers suitable to be assessors, and in conducting assessor training.
- In eschewing potential bias the assessment centre process as a whole must be examined (Alban-Metcalfe 1989).
- The competencies may reflect a 'male', or 'textbook', model of management. The job analysis stage is therefore critical in ensuring 'representativeness' of women and ethnic minorities, and in accurately reflecting the job as it is currently *performed*.

5 *The cost*: One of the biggest disadvantages associated with assessment centres is their expense, particularly in comparison to an assessment method such as the interview. Having said this we have already described that 'utility values' measuring the cost-effectiveness of the process are extremely high for assessment centres. However there are a number of ways that costs can be reduced without decreasing – and in some cases enhancing (Adler 1987) – the validity of the procedure; for example: eliminating the 'consensus' meeting where all assessors agree ratings in favour of a 'mechanical' strategy; abandoning the leaderless group discussion which has little fidelity to real work situations in favour of role-play simulations; concentrating on simulation exercises only; administering exercises through the post or the telephone; and presentations made to simulated audiences video-taped for later evaluation by assessors (see Lyons *et al.* 1993).

Such innovative moves are under way in evaluating and developing US principals; for example, at the Centre for Assessment of Administrative Performance (Bolton 1990), and at Texas A & M University (Erlandson 1990).

The Future for Assessment Centres

The assessment centre process has its origins in the identification of leadership potential in the pre-war German military effort and during the second world war by the British War Office Selection Board (Blanksby and Iles 1990). They were created in response to a set of historical and situational demands, focusing primarily on accuracy. Factors such as how decisions are made, ensuring the participant's understanding and agreement of the process and its recommendations, providing cumulative and comprehensive feedback, and keeping costs low in improving efficiency were not key issues to those responsible for the design and running of the centres. The current needs of both public and private sector organizations, however, are very different from those which led to the design of the original centres (Griffiths and Allen 1987). Despite the changed economic, social, and political contexts in which organizations now function, assessment centres are still generally constructed along 'traditional' lines.

The challenge for the future is clear. Assessment centres need to be refocused to meet the demands of the current environment. They will need to be cost-effective and efficient, and have the capability of assessment for development purposes, i.e. to be development rather than assessment centres. Allied to this the assessment centre must be viewed as part of a total ongoing selection or management development process, rather than as an end in itself, operating in conjunction with quality control and monitoring of the system as a whole (Lyons *et al*. 1993).

As well as having a positive effect on candidates, assessment centres may have a negative impact on participants. If insensitively administered they may produce feelings of reduced self-esteem, or conversely the creation of an overinflated sense of worth, leading to complacency (Fletcher C. 1991). This may be avoided by the provision of feedback after the centre which is neither pejorative nor laudatory but supportive. It is also imperative that an individual's assessment of competence is supported by a series of development programmes capable of addressing a shortfall in a particular competency, although the extent to which each competency can be developed will vary. The latter needs to be seen as integral and not as an adjunct to the assessment centre process. Blanksby and Iles (1990) show that follow up actions do not have to be restricted to traditional training solutions but can take the form of managers acting as coaches and mentors (discussed below), the drawing up of learning contracts, secondments and so forth.

Self-Evaluation Using the Headteacher Management Competencies

Several arguments favouring the use of self-evaluation in supporting competency-based development and training and appraisal have been made (see Chapter 2, Section 3, and above), for example, the accuracy of the assessment, particularly where it is combined with the views of others, and the sense of individual ownership and responsibility engendered by the process. Gane and Morgan (1992) state in reference to self-appraisal that the process by its very nature forces those who make use of it to question in a systematic way what they do and how they do it.

There is always the danger of an individual undertaking the process to do so in a perfunctory manner, or lead to self-assessments which are unduly harsh or lenient. However research has indicated that people are generally accurate in assessing their own behaviour (Mabe and West 1982).

Headteacher management competencies derived here provide an excellent source of self-evaluation for headteachers. A self-evaluation pro forma for use by head-teachers, and/or deputy headteachers, and possibly other senior staff in schools, is attached in Appendix 6. This document, based on the headteacher management competencies presented earlier in Chapter 4, is in the form of a management development exercise.

A self-evaluation exercise may be used by heads and deputy heads:

- to identify areas of the present job or the next job where skills can be developed further, as well as training needs;
- to identify areas of particular personal interest as well as those of low interest indicating personal motivation;
- to compare the self-ratings with performance ratings provided independently by a 'critical friend' (i.e. a peer, superordinate or subordinate; see section below the 360 degree approach);
- to use the respective completed pro formas to discuss and agree face to face with the critical friend an overall performance rating for each competency;
- to agree points of strength and points for development leading to a training and development action plan.

All ratings should be backed up by explicit evidence or concrete examples of 'something which went well' and/or 'something which went less well'. It is essential that both the job holder and the critical friend can provide such evidence.

The job holder's interest rating given to a competency will give an indication of personal motivation, intimating the desire to pursue an identified development need. In this way incongruity between required development needs and personal motivation may be explored.

A number of developmental priorities, usually between two and four, will need to be clearly specified in any development plan. For each developmental priority this may take the form of a statement of:

- the development need;
- the action to be taken;
- the standard to be achieved and indicative evidence produced;
- the proposed review and date; and
- required follow-up action.

A pro forma is provided for this purpose in Appendix 6.

The headteacher competencies are flexible in their use for self-evaluation, and should be recast according to individual needs. The competencies may be ranked at the beginning of the exercise according to their importance

- for the priorities of school development; or
- for the priorities of individual career development; or
- for personal interest.

The self-evaluation procedure will be most effective where there is a genuinely supporting yet challenging discussion between the job holder and the critical friend.

The 360 Degree Approach to Developing and Assessing Headteachers

While there may be certain circumstances where self-evaluation alone is considered appropriate, in many situations the comparison of self-ratings with a separate evaluation made by others will be of additional value. For example, it will

* add further rigour and objectivity to the process;
* involve others in the organization in the evaluation process;
* present a more comprehensive view of the job holder's performance; and
* be valuable to the job holder in highlighting job areas where the job holder's own perceptions of their behaviour diverge from the perceptions of others.

An exemplar was provided of the use of a critical friend to supplement self-assessment. The critical friend may be a peer, a superordinate, or a subordinate. Assessment and feedback by a number of such providers, in combination with the individual's self-evaluation, is termed the 360 degree approach to assessing and developing headteachers.

In this approach assessment may be by a combination of:

1 *Downward appraisal* from an individual to whom the head 'reports' on a regular basis, for example a senior LEA inspector, the chair of governors, or an experienced headteacher colleague acting as mentor.
2 *Peer appraisal* from one or more headteacher colleagues with whom there is sufficient direct and ongoing contact to ensure an accurate assessment by them of the head's behaviour in school.
3 *Upwards appraisal*, for example, by the deputy head, another member of the senior management team, or other school staff. Political considerations and the potentially sensitive nature of this form of evaluation may mean that the appraiser, and most likely also the appraisee, seek appraiser anonymity. Saville and Holdsworth (1993b) strongly recommend that subordinate ratings are gathered from a minimum of three people and aggregated into a single profile for feedback to the job holder, thereby safeguarding confidentiality of appraisers while augmenting objectivity.
4 *Group discussions* represent an innovative option which allows more than one peer, subordinate or superordinate to have an input by discussing and agreeing by consensus the rating to be given (Saville and Holdsworth 1993b), although precautions may have to be taken in guarding against forceful personalities influencing ratings assigned.

The amalgam of self-assessment and assessment by others is also likely to be enhanced where the relationship between the critical friend and the job holder takes the form of a mentoring partnership, to which we now turn our attention.

The Use of a Mentoring Partner

A mentor is a more experienced individual willing to share his/her knowledge with someone less experienced, in a relationship of mutual trust. A mixture of parent and peer, the mentor's primary function is to be a transitional figure in an individual's development. (Clutterbuck, 1992)

The individual's skills and abilities in terms of competencies may be developed and improved through the effective use of a mentoring relationship. By its relatively low cost, and its ability to facilitate learning and development in a non-threatening manner, it is seen as particularly attractive to many organizations. Indeed some organizations formalize the process through the drawing up of a mentoring contract, and covering important issues such as the confidentiality of the process, the review of the job holder's progress etc.

The process does not have to be quite so prescribed. Headteachers and other staff in schools may enter into a mentoring partnership which is not formalized. Nevertheless it is important to aim for the benefits to be offered by mentoring provision.

The benefits for headteachers entering into a mentoring relationship with, for example, a peer, would include: help and guidance in dealing with specific difficult situations by referring to an experienced practitioner, particularly for a new head in adjusting to the demands of the new job; and in acting as a source of advice on personal development needs and career development. This has the advantages of economizing on more formalized training and development, and increasing the motivation and job satisfaction of both the head and the mentor. For his or her part the mentor will gain new perspectives which may challenge his or her present practice, possibly effecting improvements, for example, in updating job knowledge and skills, and also in gaining insights into motivating and developing the mentor's own staff in school.

The key role of the mentor – in 'coaching', 'counselling', 'facilitating' and 'networking' (Clutterbuck 1992) – expedite a number of key mentor functions. These lie primarily in:

- helping the job holder to use work events and situations to identify work areas of personal strength and areas where development might be required;
- setting clear learning targets to improve targeted competencies;
- helping the job holder to establish career goals and a career path by which these goals might be realized;
- coaching the job holder to improve managerial skills;

- handing down knowledge, as well as informing job holders, particularly new headteachers, of attitudes and perspectives which might be adopted in handling new situations, and in adapting to a senior managerial role; and
- being a source of advice and support to the head by listening and providing constructive feedback.

Summary and Conclusions

The advantages to be derived from the adoption of a competence-based approach to the recruitment and selection, to the management development and training, and to the appraisal of headteachers have been highlighted. Of particular advantage is the improvement of the effectiveness of selection and recruitment systems in schools, and in justifying the fairness of the system.

As regards management development, the efficacy of competence-based systems in diagnosing training needs, and fostering and supporting personal responsibility for development and training, have been identified, and also the necessity to link motivational and career issues to the objective assessment of skill and competency development needs. Competencies are also shown to be a means of supporting headteacher appraisal, particularly in self-appraisal.

While competencies are used in selection and recruitment, training, and appraisal processes, the primary focus in using competencies is to improve one key stage in these processes, that of diagnosis and assessment. The fundamental focus is therefore competency-based assessment.

The assessment centre process, built on competencies and work-relevant exercises derived from job analysis, and using multiple assessors, is presented as the most accurate and valid measure currently available to assess headteacher competence. While the process has some drawbacks, for example the cost of the process and assessor error, overall it has the advantages of flexibility and variety of use; face, content, and predictive validity; a high return on investment; and the ability to address equal opportunities issues. The challenge for the future lies in refocusing assessment centres to the demands of the current environment, for example in being cost-effective and efficient, assessing for development rather than selection, and being part of an ongoing development process.

The assessment centre represents a sophisticated technique for assessing headteacher competence. The use of the headteacher management competencies derived from this research, in a self-evaluation exercise (as attached in Appendix 6), presents for heads an inexpensive, readily available, and extremely effective tool for assessing competence.

The 360 degree approach has been suggested as being of use to heads in supplementing their self-evaluation, that is, through the possible addition of downward appraisal, peer appraisal, upwards appraisal and group discussions. Additionally, the benefits to heads of forming a mentoring partnership with, for example, an experienced peer, have been highlighted.

Chapter 6

Conclusions

The principal focus of this book has been to demonstrate a methodology which can provide rigorously produced and objective criteria to underpin the assessment decision making process. The assessment is for use for management development and training purposes, for recruitment and selection, or for appraisal.

To do this we advocate the use of techniques widely adopted in non-educational employment sectors but hitherto not systematically adopted within education. Our particular focus has been upon the position of headteachers of maintained schools although the techniques are equally applicable across the educational sectors. Those techniques we advocate are job analysis, to provide an accurate and replicable picture of the head's job now and, derived from the data produced by this process, the generation and validation of management competencies to provide the criteria upon which objective assessment decision making is based.

The data was produced by undertaking job analysis, and generating and developing management competencies as part of a national research project. This involved the participation of headteachers drawn from schools across England and Wales. The techniques of data collection and analysis used in the research were developed by Saville and Holdsworth Ltd. and their systematic use with such large numbers of headteachers in Britain is reported for the first time.

Summaries are provided at the end of each chapter of the book. Part I presented the underpinning theoretical framework adopted in the book. Chapter 1 outlined to the reader the various theoretical approaches to job analysis which might be used. A behavioural/task related approach was identified as being most appropriate to an analysis of the job of headteacher.

Chapter 2 provided a theoretical framework underpinning the development, validation and use of management competencies. The two main approaches to management competencies usage, the occupational standards approach (NVQs) and the personal qualities approach are outlined. Adopted here as more appropriate to the managerial activities of senior managers is a personal qualities approach which focuses on transferable competencies.

Two self-report questionnaires developed by Saville and Holdsworth Ltd were used to collect job analysis data. The Work Profiling System (WPS) was used in a group context where heads freely discussed with each other all aspects of the questionnaire and their selection of particular items. Also, a personality questionnaire specifically designed for use in an occupational context, the Occupational Personality Questionnaire (OPQ) enabled heads to identify their preferred ways of working.

Intensive school-based interviewing using repertory grid and critical incident analysis was conducted to provide additional job analysis information.

Part II of the book comprises Chapter 3 and reports the results of the job analysis research, first, the data relating to the Occupational Personality Questionnaire, and second, to the Work Profiling System. This is then used to present the first picture of the head's job comprising a prioritized job description, and a headteacher person specification. Some of the difficulties and dilemmas for assessment emerging from the research are also identified.

Part III of the book focuses on the outcomes of relevance from the research to assessing and developing headteachers. Chapter 4 demonstrates how from the data provided by job analysis management competencies are generated and validated. The headteacher management competencies derived from the research are presented, encapsulating the essential features of headship at the present time. Competencies produced in different circumstances for various occupational sectors are presented for comparison purposes.

Chapter 5 provides an overview of the various commonly adopted approaches to competency-led assessment. Assessment centre use was identified as providing the most objective means of assessment currently available. However, its disadvantages which relate particularly to resourcing and cost were acknowledged. For heads and schools, self-evaluation underpinned by the headteacher management competencies derived from the research may provide an inexpensive but extremely powerful process for assessment.

A Research Agenda

In common with many research projects as many questions seem to be thrown up by the research as there are answers provided. Section 4 in Chapter 3 on difficulties and dilemmas for the head begins to identify a number of these. Those which relate to headteacher effectiveness and to school effectiveness also provide an example. In the climate of effectiveness, efficiency and accountability that presently prevails, independent measures of predictive validity appear as elusive as ever. Differences between school phases and between preferred styles of working identified by gender raise the issues of long and short term effectiveness of performance, raising the prospect that differentially applicable training regimes may be necessary.

One of the major aims of the work was to justify the use of the approach and of the techniques adopted here, to demonstrate their utility and applicability, in order that others may emulate the methodology. The research process has the advantage of being replicable, permitting meaningful comparisons to be undertaken between educational leaders working in different contexts, across occupational barriers, and also in the conduct of cross-cultural studies. Additionally, given the changed nature of educational leadership, the opportunity of investigating change over a period of time through a longitudinal approach also becomes possible.

The issue is not one of the imposition of techniques alien to the education sector, but of understanding how other non-educational employment sectors resolve similar problems. The substantial legislative changes which have been imposed upon the educational system entail that school governors are accountable for assessment decision making, particularly for the appointment of headteachers. School governors may or may not appreciate the significance of the legislative changes made to the system in the last decade and particularly the impact that these changes have had upon the job of the headteacher. We recognize that the sophistication of the techniques we are proposing may interpose a barrier to their easy adoption in individual schools. While school governors may take our recommendations and findings on trust, whether or not an appointment to a head's post turns out to be appropriate, they will nevertheless still remain accountable for the assessment decision.

We recognize the dilemmas our work raises. If 'outside experts' are not to be employed then the use of our work to influence in-school decision making is a way forward. The techniques that we advocate and the data they produce provide an insightful and profitable direction for the educational sector to follow.

References

ADAIR, J. (1988) *The Action-Centred Leader*, London: The Industrial Society.

ADAIR, J. (1990) *Understanding Motivation*, Guildford: The Talbot Adair Press.

ADLER, S. (1987) 'Toward the more efficient use of assessment centre technology in personnel selection', *Journal of Business and Psychology*, **2**(1): 74–93.

ADLER, S., LANEY, J. and PACKER, M. (1993) *Managing Women*, Buckingham: Open University Press.

ALBAN-METCALFE, B. (1989) 'The use of assessment centres in the NHS', report published by the National Health Service Training Agency.

ARGYRIS, C. and SCHON, D. (1978) *Theory Into Practice: Increasing Professional Effectiveness*, San Francisco, CA: Jossey-Bass.

ASHWORTH, P.D. and SAXTON, J. (1990) 'On competence', *Journal of Further and Higher Education*, **14**(2): 3–25.

AUDIT COMMISSION (1991) *Management Within Primary Schools*, London: HMSO.

BASS, B.M. (1981) *Stogdill's Handbook of Leadership: A Survey of Theory and Research*, Glencoe: Free Press.

BAWTREE, S. and HOGG, C. (1989) 'Assessment centres', *Personnel Management*, Factsheet 22, October.

BELBIN, R.M. (1981) *Management Teams: Why They Succeed or Fail*, Oxford: Heinemann Professional Publishing Ltd.

BETHELL-FOX, C.E. (1989) 'Psychological testing', in P. HERRIOT (ed.) *Assessment and Selection in Organisations*, Chichester: Wiley.

BLACK, H. and WOLF, A. (eds) (1990) *Knowledge and Competence: Current Issues in Training and Education*, Sheffield: Employment Department.

BLANKSBY, B. and ILES, P. (1990) 'Recent developments in assessment centre theory, practice, and operation', *Personnel Review*, **19**(6): 33–44.

BLINKHORN, S. and JOHNSON, C. (1990) 'The insignificance of personality testing', *Nature*, **348**: 671–2.

BOAK, G. (1991) *Developing Managerial Competences: The Management Learning Contract Approach*, London: Pitman.

BOAM, R. and SPARROW, P. (eds) (1992) *Designing and Achieving Competency*, Maidenhead, Berkshire: McGraw Hill.

BOLTON, D. (1990) *Recent Developments in Methodology for Administrator Assessment Centres. Conceptual Changes and Their Implications for Performance Assessment*, Seattle, WA: University of Washington.

BOYATZIS, R. (1982) *The Competent Manager*, New York: Wiley.

BOYATZIS, R.E. and KOLB, D.A. (1991) 'Assessing individuality in learning: The learning skills profile', *Educational Psychology*, **11**(3, 4): 279–95.

BOYATZIS, R.E. and KOLB, D.A. (1992) 'Modes of growth and adaptation throughout career and life', paper presented at the Eleventh International Training and Development Conference, Management Centre Europe, June.

BRAY, D.W. (1982) 'The assessment center and the study of lives', *American Psychologist*, **37**: 180–9.

CALDWELL, B.J. (1994) 'Leading the transformation of Australia's schools', *Educational Management and Administration*, **22**(2): 76–84.

CALDWELL, B.J. and SPINKS, J.M. (1988) *The Self-Managing School*, London: Falmer Press.

CASCIO, W.F. and SILBEY, V. (1979) 'Utility of the assessment centre as a selection device', *Journal of Applied Psychology*, **64**: 107–18.

CLERKIN, C. (1985) 'What do primary heads actually do all day?', *School Organisation*, **5**(4): 287–300.

CLUTTERBUCK, D. (1992) *Mentoring Kit*, Henley-on-Thames: Henley Distance Learning Ltd.

CNAA/BTEC (1990) *The Assessment of Management Competencies: Project Report*, London: CNAA.

COOPER, C.L. and KELLY, M.J. (1993) 'Occupational stress in headteachers: A national study', *British Journal of Educational Psychology*, **63**: 130–43.

DALE, M. and ILES, P. (1992) *Assessing Management Skills: A Guide to Competencies and Evaluation Techniques*, London: Kogan Page.

DULEWICZ, V. (1989) 'Assessment centres as the route to competence', *Personnel Management*, **21**(11) November: 56–9.

EARLEY, P. (1992) *The School Management Competencies Project* (3 volumes), Crawley: School Management South.

EARLEY, P. (1993) 'Developing competence in schools: A critique of standards-based approaches to management development', *Educational Management and Administration*, **21**(4): 233–44.

EDWARDS, S. and LYONS, G. (1994) 'Female secondary headteachers – An endangered species?', *Management in Education*, **8**(2): 7–10.

ELLIOTT, J. (1989) 'Appraisal of performance or persons', in H. SIMMONS and J. ELLIOTT (eds) *Rethinking Appraisal and Assessment*, Milton Keynes: Open University Press.

EMPLOYMENT DEPARTMENT (1994) *The Place of Knowledge and Understanding in the Development of National Vocational Qualifications and Scottish Vocational Qualifications*, Competence and Assessment Briefing Series, No. 10, October.

EMPLOYMENT DEPARTMENT LEARNING METHODS BRANCH (1994) *Ethics in Occupational Standards, NVQs and SVQs. Research and Development Series*, Report No. 22, June.

ERAUT, M. (1990) 'Identifying the knowledge which underpins performance', in H. BLACK and A. WOLF (eds) *Knowledge and Competence: Current Issues in Training and Education*, Sheffield: Employment Department.

ERLANDSON, D. *et al.* (1990) 'The management profile', in D. ERLANDSON (ed.) *The Principal in the 1990s*, Tempe, AZ: UCEA.

ERLANDSON, D. and LYONS, G. (1995) 'The jobs of British primary headteachers and texas elementary principals', *The Journal of School Leadership*, **5**, September, 418–47.

ESP, D. (1993) *Competencies for School Managers*, London: Kogan Page.

EVERARD, B. (1990) 'A critique of the MCI/TA/NCVQ competency approach as applied to education management', *Educational Change and Development*, **11**(1): 15–16.

EVERARD, K.B. (1988) *Developing Management in Schools*, Oxford: Basil Blackwell.

FELTHAM, R. (1992) 'Using competencies in selection and recruitment', in R. BOAM and P. SPARROW (eds) *Designing and Achieving Competency*, Maidenhead, Berkshire: McGraw Hill.

FIDLER, B. and COOPER, R. (1992) (eds) *Staff Appraisal and Staff Management in Schools and Colleges: A Guide to Implementation*, Harlow: Longman.

FLANAGAN, J.C. (1954) 'The critical incident technique', *Psychological Bulletin*, **51**(4): 327–58.

FLETCHER, C. (1991) 'Candidates' reactions to assessment centres and their outcomes: A longitudinal study', *Journal of Occupational Psychology*, **64**: 117–27.

FLETCHER, C. (1993) *Appraisal: Routes to Improved Performance*, London: Institute of Personnel Management.

FLETCHER, C. *et al.* (1991) 'Personality tests: The great debate', *Personnel Management*, September: 38–42.

FLETCHER, S. (1991) *Designing Competence-Based Training*, London: Kogan Page.

FULLAN, M. (with STIEGELBAUER, S.) (1991) *The New Meaning of Educational Change*, London: Cassell.

FURNHAM, A. (1992) *Personality at Work: The Role of Individual Differences in the Work Place*, London: Routledge.

GAEL, S. (1983) *Job Analysis: A Guide to Assessing Work Activities*, London: Jossey-Bass.

GAEL, S. (ed.) (1987) *The Job Analysis Handbook for Business, Industry and Government*, Chichester: John Wiley and Sons.

GANE, V. and MORGAN, A. (1992) *Managing Headteacher Appraisal*, London: Paul Chapman.

GAUGLER, B., ROSENTHAL, D.B., THORNTON, G.C. III and BENTSON, C. (1987) 'Meta-analysis of assessment centre validity', *Journal of Applied Psychology*, **72**(3): 493–511.

GHORPADE, J.V. (1988) *Job Analysis: A Handbook for the Human Resource Director*, Prentice-Hall.

GRAY, H.L. (1987) 'Gender considerations in school management: Masculine and feminine leadership styles', *School Organisation*, **7**(3): 7–19.

GRIFFITHS, P. and ALLEN, B. (1987) 'Assessment centres: Breaking with tradition', *Journal of Management Development*, **6**(1): 18–29.

HANDY, C.B. (1981) *Understanding Organisations*, 2nd edn, London: Penguin.

HERRIOT, P. (ed.) (1989) *Assessment and Selection in Organisations*, Chichester: Wiley.

HOGAN, J. and ZENKE, L.L. (1986) 'Dollar-value utility of alternative procedures for selecting school principals', *Educational and Psychological Measurement*, **46**: 935–45.

HOOGHIEMSTRA, T. (1992) 'Integrated management of human resources', in A. MITRANI, M. DALZIEL and D. FITT (eds) *Competency Based Human Resource Management*, London: Kogan Page.

HUBA, G.J. and MELCHIOR, L.A. (1989) *Job Analysis, Development and Validation of Psychological Evaluations of Candidates for Protective Service Worker Positions*, report by the Measurement Group, Department of Social Services, San Diego County, CA.

HUCK, J.R. and BRAY, D.W. (1976) 'Management assessment centre evaluations and subsequent job performance on white and black females', *Personnel Psychology*, **29**: 13–30.

JACKSON, D. and ROTHSTEIN, M. (1993) 'Evaluating personality testing in personnel selection', *The Psychologist: Bulletin of the British Psychological Society*, **6**: 8–11.

JACOBS, R. (1989) 'Getting the measure of managerial competence', *Personnel Management*, **21**(10), October: 80–85.

JACOBS, R.C. and VYAKARNAM, S. (1994) 'The need for a more strategically led, research-based approach in management development', paper presented at the Occupational Psychology Conference, Birmingham, January.

JAFFEE, C.L. and SEFCIK, J.T. JR (1980) 'What is an assessment centre?', *The Personnel Administrator*, 40–43, February.

JENKINS, H.O. (1985) 'Job perceptions of senior managers in schools and manufacturing industry', *Educational Management and Administration*, **13**(1): 1–11.

JENKINS, H.O. (1991) *Getting It Right; A Handbook for Successful School Leadership*, Oxford: Basil Blackwell.

JIRASINGHE, D.J. (1994) 'Management competencies for headteachers: A job analysis of tasks and occupational personality characteristics', doctoral thesis, University of East London, September.

JIRASINGHE, D.J. and LYONS, G. (1995) 'Managerial competencies in action: A practical framework', *School Organisation*, **15**(3): 267–81.

JOHNSTON, J. (1986) 'Gender differences in teachers' preferences for primary school leadership', *Educational Management and Administration*, **14**(3): 219–26.

JONES, A. (1987) *Leadership for Tomorrow's Schools*, Oxford: Basil Blackwell.

KELLY, G. (1955) *The Psychology of Personal Constructs, Vol. 1, A Theory of Personality*, New York: W.W. Norton & Co. Ltd.

KLEMP, G.O., JR (1979) 'On the identification, measurement, and integration of competence', in M. KEETON and P. POTTINGER (eds) *Competence: The Concept, its Measurability and Implications for Licensing, Certification, and Education*, San Francisco, CA: Jossey-Bass.

KLEMP, G.O., JR (1980) *The Assessment of Occupational Competence*, report to the National Institute of Education, Washington, DC.

KLINE, P. (1992) *Psychometric Testing in Personnel Selection and Appraisal*, Kingston: Kroner.

KLINE, P. (1993) *Personality: The Psychometric View*. London: Routledge.

KNOTT, B. (1975) 'What is a competence-based curriculum in the liberal arts?' *Journal of Higher Education*, **46**(1): 25–39.

LEVINE, E. *et al.* (1983) 'Evaluation of job analysis methods by experienced job analysts', *Academy of Management Journal*, **26**: 339–48.

LONDON BOROUGH OF KENSINGTON AND CHELSEA/HAY MANAGEMENT CONSULTANTS (1990) *The Competencies of an Effective Head Teacher*, project report, April.

LORENZO, R.V. (1984) 'Effects of assessorship on managers' proficiency in acquiring, evaluating, and communicating information about people', *Personnel Psychology*, **37**: 617–34.

LYONS, G. (1974) *The Administrative Tasks of Heads and Senior Staff in Large Secondary Schools*, Bristol: University of Bristol.

LYONS, G. (1976) *Heads' Tasks: A Handbook of Secondary School Administration*, Slough: NFER Publishing Co.

LYONS, G. and JIRASINGHE, D. (1992) 'Headteachers' assessment and development centres', *Educational Change and Development*, **13**(1): 3–5.

LYONS, G., JIRASINGHE, D.J., EWERS, C. and EDWARDS, S. (1993) 'The development of a headteachers' assessment centre', *Educational Management and Administration*, **21**(4): 245–8.

LYONS, G. and JIRASINGHE, D.J. (1994) *The Headteachers Research Project*, ELBS, University of East London.

MABE, P.A. and WEST, S.G. (1982) 'Validity of self-evaluation of ability: A review and meta-analysis', *Journal of Applied Psychology*, **67**: 280–96.

MCCLEARY, L.E. (1973) 'Competency-based educational administration and applications to related fields', research paper, Salt Lake City, UT: University of Utah, January.

MCCLEARY, L.E. (1984) 'Knowledge, competence, performance: Meanings and values to an applied professional field', *CCBC Notebook*, pp. 3–9, July.

MCCLEARY, L.E. and OGAWA, R. (1989) 'The assessment centre process for selecting school leaders', *School Organisation*, **9**(1): 103–13.

MCCLEARY, L.E. *et al.* (1978) *The Senior High School Principalship: The National Survey*, Reston, VA: National Association of Secondary School Principals.

MCCLELLAND, D.C. (1973) 'Testing for competence rather than for "intelligence"', *American Psychologist*, **28**(1): 1–4.

MCCORMICK, E.J. (1976) 'Job and task analysis', in M.V. DUNNETTE (ed.) *Handbook of Industrial and Organizational Psychology*, Chicago, IL: Rand McNally.

MANAGEMENT CHARTER INITIATIVE (MCI) (1990) *Assessment Guidelines*, London: MCI.

MANASSE, A.L. (1985) 'Improving conditions for principal effectiveness: Policy implications of research', *The Elementary School Journal*, **85**(3): 339–63.

MANSFIELD, B. (1990) 'Knowledge, evidence and assessment', in H. BLACK and

A. WOLF (eds) *Knowledge and Competence: Current Issues in Training and Education*, Sheffield: Employment Department.

MARTINKO, W. and GARDNER, W. (1983) *The Behavior of High Performing Educational Managers: An Observational Study*, Tallahassee, FL: Florida State University.

MEDLEY, D.M., ROSENBLUM, E.P. and VANCE, N.C. (1989) 'Assessing the functional knowledge of participants in the Virginia Beginning Teacher Assistance Program', *The Elementary School Journal*, **89**(4): 495–510.

MORGAN, C., HALL, V. and MACKAY, H. (1983) *The Selection of Secondary School Headteachers*, Milton Keynes: Open University Press.

MORGAN, C., HALL, V. and MACKAY, H. (1984) *A Handbook on Selecting Senior Staff for Schools*, Milton Keynes: Open University Press.

MORTIMORE, P., SAMMONS, P., STOLL, L., LEWIS, D. and ECOB, R. (1988) *School Matters: The Junior Years*, Wells: Open Books.

MOSES, J.L. and BYHAM, W.C. (1977) *Applying the Assessment Centre Method*, New York: Pergamon Press.

NATIONAL EDUCATIONAL ASSESSMENT CENTRE (NEAC) (1995) *The Competencies*, Oxford Brooks University: NEAC.

NIAS, J., SOUTHWORTH, G. and YEOMANS, R. (1989) *Understanding the Primary School as an Organisation*, London: Holt, Rinehart and Winston.

OLIVER, J. (1992) 'The NEAC competency-based assessment for heads and deputies', paper presented at the British Education Management and Administration Society (BEMAS) Annual Conference, Bristol, September.

OUSTON, J. (1991) 'What does the competency approach have to offer to the development of managers in education?' paper presented to the BEMAS Management Development Group, Management Competencies and School Effectiveness Workshop, Birmingham, December.

OZGA, J. (1993) *Women in Educational Management*, Buckingham: Open University Press.

PEARN, M. and KANDOLA, R. (1988) *Job Analysis: A Practical Guide For Managers*, 1st edn, Crawley: Institute of Personnel Management.

PEARN, M. and KANDOLA, R. (1993) *Job Analysis: A Manager's Guide*, 2nd, edn, London: Institute of Personnel Management.

PETERS, T.J. and WATERMAN, R.H. (1982) *In Search Of Excellence*, New York: Harper and Row.

PIPES, M. (1990) 'What makes a good secondary head?' *NUT Educational Review*, Autumn: 44–5.

REBER, A.S. (1985) *Penguin Dictionary of Psychology*, London: Penguin.

REES, R. (1989) 'Can you improve your selection methods?' *Works Management*, February: 42–7.

RIBBINS, P. (1994) *Headship Matters*, Harlow, Essex: Longman.

ROBERTSON, I.T. and KINDER, A. (1993) 'Personality and job competencies: The criterion-related validity of some personality variables', *Journal of Occupational and Organisational Psychology*, **66**(3): 225–44.

SACKETT, P. R. and DREHER, G.F. (1982) 'Constructs and assessment centre dimensions: Some troubling empirical findings', *Journal of Applied Psychology*, **67**: 401–10.

SACKETT, P.R. and HAKEL, M.D. (1979) 'Temporal stability and individual differences in using assessment information to form overall ratings', *Organisational Behaviour and Human Performance*, **23**: 120–37.

SASHKIN, M. (1991) 'Strategic leadership competencies, what are they? How do they operate? What can be done to develop them?' draft prepared for the Strategic Leadership Conference Co-sponsored by the Army War College, Army Research Institute, and Texas Tech University, USA February.

SAVILLE AND HOLDSWORTH (1990a) *OPQ Manual*, Thames Ditton, Surrey: SHL.

SAVILLE AND HOLDSWORTH (1990b) *WPS Manual*, Thames Ditton, Surrey: SHL.

SAVILLE AND HOLDSWORTH (1990c) *Practical Job Analysis*, Thames Ditton, Surrey: SHL.

SAVILLE AND HOLDSWORTH (1991) *OPQ Update 1*, Thames Ditton, Surrey: SHL.

SAVILLE AND HOLDSWORTH (1992) *OPQ Update, OPQ British Standardisation Study: Report Number 2, Age, Gender, and Personality*, January, Thames Ditton, Surrey: SHL.

SAVILLE AND HOLDSWORTH (1993a) *OPQ Update, Updating the OPQ Series*, October, Thames Ditton, Surrey: SHL.

SAVILLE AND HOLDSWORTH (1993b) *The IMC Manual and User's Guide*, Thames Ditton, Surrey: SHL.

SAVILLE AND HOLDSWORTH (1994) *OPQ Update, OPQ Moves into Second Decade*, April, Thames Ditton, Surrey: SHL.

SAVILLE AND HOLDSWORTH (1995) *Best Practice in the Use of Job Analysis Techniques*, Thames Ditton, Surrey: SHL.

SAVILLE, P. and MUNRO, A. (1986) 'The relationship between the factor model of the Occupational Personality Questionnaire and the 16PF', *Personnel Review*, **15**(5): 30–4.

SCHMITT, N. and HILL, T.E. (1977) 'Sex and race composition of assessment centre groups as a determinant of peer and assessor ratings', *Journal of Applied Psychology*, **62**(3): 261–4.

SCHMITT, N. *et al.* (1981) *NASSP Competencies. Validity Study*, East Lansing, MI: Michigan State University.

SCHMITT, N., GOODING, R.Z., NOE, R.A. and KIRSCH, M. (1984) 'Meta-analyses of validity studies published between 1964 and 1982 and the investigation of study characteristics', *Personnel Psychology*, **37**: 407–22.

SCHOOL MANAGEMENT SOUTH (1991) *School Management Competencies Project: Standards for School Managers*, Crawley: SMS.

SCHRODER, H.M. (1989) *Managerial Competence: The Key to Excellence*, Iowa: Kendall/Hunt.

SHAKESHAFT, C. (1987) *Women in Educational Administration*, Newbury Park, CA: Sage.

SHAKESHAFT, C. (1993) 'Women in educational management in the United States', in J. OUSTON (ed.) *Women in Education Management*, Harlow, Essex: Longman.

SMITH, M. and ROBERTSON, I. (1992) 'Assessing competencies', in R. BOAM and

P. SPARROW (eds) Designing and Achieving Competency, Maidenhead, Berkshire: McGraw Hill.

SOUTHWORTH, G. (1990) 'Leadership, headship, and effective primary schools', *School Organisation*, **10**(1): 3–16.

SPENCER, L.M. and SPENCER, S.M. (1993) *Competence at Work: Models for Superior Performance*, New York: John Wiley and Sons.

STEWART, R. (1982) *Choices for the Manager: A Guide to Managerial Work and Behavior*, New York: McGraw Hill.

TASK FORCE ON ASSESSMENT CENTRE STANDARDS (1980) 'Standards and ethical considerations for assessment centre operations', *The Personnel Administrator*, 35–38, February.

TEACHER TRAINING AGENCY (TTA) (1995) *Headlamp: An Initiative to Support Newly Appointed Headteachers*, London: Teacher Training Agency.

THOMAS, H. and BULLOCK, A. (1994) 'In search of quality time', *The Times Educational Supplement*, pp. 8–20, May.

TOPLIS, J., DULEWICZ, V. and FLETCHER, C. (1991) *Psychological Testing: A Manager's Guide*, 2nd edn, London: Institute of Personnel Management.

TRAINING AGENCY (1988) *Guidance Notes*, Sheffield: Training Agency.

TRAINING AGENCY (1989) *Guidance Notes*, Sheffield: Training Agency.

TRAINING AND DEVELOPMENT LEAD BODY (1992) *National Standards for Training and Development*. Sheffield: Employment Department.

VAILL, P. (1983) 'The theory of managing in the managerial competency movement. Exchange', *The Organisational Behaviour Teaching Journal*, **8**(2): 50–4.

WEBB, P.C. and LYONS, G. (1982) 'The nature of managerial activities in education', in H.L. GRAY (ed.) *The Management of Educational Institutions: Theory, Research and Consultancy*, London: Falmer Press.

WEINDLING, D. and EARLEY, P. (1987) *Secondary Headship: The First Years*, Windsor: NFER Nelson.

WOLCOTT, H.F. (1973) *The Man in the Principal's Office: An Ethnography*, New York: Holt, Rinehart and Winston.

WOLF, A. (1990) 'Unwrapping knowledge and understanding from standards of competence', in H. BLACK and A. WOLF (eds) *Knowledge and Competence: Current Issues in Training and Education*, Sheffield: Employment Department.

WOODRUFFE, C. (1992) 'What is meant by a competency?', in R. BOAM and P. SPARROW (eds) *Designing and Achieving Competency*, Maidenhead, Berkshire: McGraw Hill.

ZUCKERMAN, M. (1989) 'Review of sixteen personality factor questionnaire', in J.C. CONOLEY and J.J. KRAMER (eds) *The Tenth Mental Measurements Yearbook*, Lincoln, NB: Buros Institute of Mental Measurements of the University of Nebraska, 1392–4.

School and Headteacher Sampling Variables – Headteacher Research Project

Heads by gender

Male	Female	Total
113	142	255

Ethnicity of head

Caucasian	Afro-Caribbean	Asian	Other	Total
243	1	5	6	255

Number of headships

1st Headship	1 Previous	2 Previous	3+ Previous	Total
181	61	10	3	255

Number of years as head

<1 year	1–2 years	3–5 years	6–10 years	11–20+ years	Total
9	39	70	66	71	255

School sector/phase

N	N/I	I	J/I	J	P	P/N	Sec	High	Mid	F	Spec	Total
2	13	22	28	30	37	31	53	2	6	18	13	255

Key to Abbreviations

N = Nursery   Sec = Secondary
I = Infant   High = High School
J = Junior   Mid = Middle School
P = Primary   F = First School
    Spec = Special School

Heads by pupil numbers

Number of Pupils							
<100	101–200	201–300	301–400	401–500	501–600	601–700	701–800
22	62	63	37	13	7	7	7

801–900	901–1000	1001–1100	1101–1200	1201–1300	1301+	Total	
9	7	8	7	3	3	255	

Schools – Pupil gender

Boys	Girls	Mixed	Total
4	8	243	255

Local Education Authorities participating in the research were Barnet, Brent, Calderdale, Camden, Coventry, Cumbria, Essex, Greenwich, Gwent, Hertfordshire, Kirklees, Mid Glamorgan, Newham, Northumberland.

For further details on sampling, see Lyons, G. and Jirasinghe, D.J. (1994) *The Headteachers Research Project. ELBS*, University of East London.

T-Values for OPQ Dimensions, Team Types and Leadership Styles Achieving Statistical Significance in an Analysis by Gender

OPQ dimensions	T-values (p < 0.01)		T-values (p < 0.05)	
	F > M	M > F	F > M	M > F
Affiliative (R5)	−3.52			
Democratic (R8)	−2.98			
Caring (R9)	−2.68			
Data rational (T2)				2.47
Artistic (T3)	−3.85			
Behavioural (T4)	−2.98			
Detail conscious (T10)	−3.22			
Conscientious (T11)			−2.49	
Relaxed (F1)		2.80		
Worrying (F2)	−3.08			
Tough minded (F3)		3.38		
Active (F7)		4.26		
Competitive (F8)		3.81		

Note: F = Female
M = Male

Leadership style/ Team type	T-values for independent samples of gender (p < 0.001)	
	F > M	M > F
Delegative leader Minimal personal involvement. Believes in delegation of task and responsibility.		3.45
Participative leader Favours consensus decision making. Prepared to take time over decisions. Ensures involvement of all relevant individuals.	−4.62	
Consultative leader Pays genuine attention to opinions/feelings of subordinates but maintains a clear sense of task objectives and makes the final decisions.	−4.19	
Team Type		
Completer Worries about problems. Personally checks details. Intolerant of the casual and slapdash. Sees projects through.	−3.16*	
Team worker Promotes team harmony. Good listener who builds on the ideas of others. Likeable and unassertive.	−5.22	

Note: * Significant to p < 0.01

F-Ratios for Significant One-Way Analysis of Variance Measures, Conducted on Personality Scales by School Sector

OPQ Scale	F-ratio values with degrees of freedom 3 and 225; $p < 0.05$	
	S > P	P > S
Data rational	2.93	
Conscientious	4.43	
Competitive	4.40	
Achieving	2.54	
Implementer	2.56	
Team worker		3.26

Note: S = Secondary
      P = Primary

Factors Elicited from Critical Incidents and Repertory Grid Interviews as Being Critical to Successful Headteacher Job Performance

Critical incident and repertory grid interviews were conducted separately from the research sessions using the Work Profiling and Personality questionnaires. All were conducted as one-to-one interviews by job analysts trained in the use of such techniques. Interviews lasted anywhere from one up to two hours, and were conducted either with heads in school, or with inspectors/advisers usually at a local authority professional development centre. Standardized interviewing procedures were adopted by all job analysts.

Critical incident interviews were undertaken with headteachers, including heads from all the major school sectors. *Repertory grid interviews* were conducted with inspectors/advisers, representing both primary and secondary school sectors.

Analysis of interviews has produced a summary of those headteacher characteristics, abilities, skills, etc. seen by heads and inspectors to differentiate successful from less successful job performance. This information is presented below and is as inclusive as possible and uses terminology and phraseology taken from the original interviews. The information was used, along with the other job analysis data, to derive the headteacher management competencies.

Implementing/Coordinating	Appraising/Evaluating
Management of curricula, budget, staff, procedures Balancing needs of individual with organization needs Time management Trouble shooting Allocating resources Finishing and completing	Monitoring progress Making evaluations Recognition of success in self and others Observing Patience, tact and diplomacy Team work Creating confidence
Planning	**Assessing/Evaluating**
Future orientation/vision Mission/strategies Strategic leadership Short term planning/setting targets Anticipating and situational analysis Flexibility Judgment Logical/systematic reasoning Diagnosis/recognition of progress	Seeking information Critical of information/self/others Political awareness/context Setting standards (self/others/procedures) Working in a given structure
Presenting/Communicating	**Motivating**
Having credibility/honesty Self-confidence Commitment Tenacity Enthusiasm/energy High visibility Making a case appropriate to audience (written and verbal) Thinking on one's feet/fluency	Participative decision making Establishing climate/tone Motivating others Mobilizing others Trust Facilitating Building esteem Need for excellence/achievement Staff development Wider personal interests/ability to switch off
Counselling/Assisting/Caring	**Learning/Researching**
Providing feedback and praise Counselling Sensitivity Reassurance and support Listening Availability Empathy	Knowledge of job/policies, etc. Philosophy of education Professional/ethical beliefs Self-motivation Generating ideas Organizational development
Controlling/Directing	**PR/Developing relationships**
Taking responsibility Deciding/directness Delegating	Persuading and negotiating Handling conflict Selling/marketing Politically adept Building and using networks

Appendix 5

Examples of Different Competencies for Headteachers and for Managers in General

---

Kensington and Chelsea Competencies (from Royal London Borough of Kensington and Chelsea, Education Department Hay Management Consultants 1990)

Competency Clusters

Core values
Vision
Achievement/Need for Excellence
Self-confidence/image/impact
Educational expertise

Creating a favourable environment
Networking
Influencing strategies
Communicating

Planning/Decision making
Initiative
Gathering/analyzing information
Learning from experience
Having perspective
Effective decision making

Managing people
Sensitivity
Persuasion
Developing others
Self-control

Implementing
Flexible management style
Determination

The National Association of Secondary School Principals' (NASSP) Competencies (from Schmitt et al. 1981)

1 *Problem analysis*
Ability to seek out relevant data and analyze complex information to determine the important elements of a problem situation; searching for information with a purpose.

137

2 *Judgment*

Ability to reach logical conclusions and make high quality decisions based on available information; skill in identifying educational needs and setting priorities; ability to evaluate written communications critically.

3 *Organizational ability*

Ability to plan, schedule, and control the work of others; skill in using resources in an optimal fashion; ability to deal with a volume of paperwork and heavy demands on one's time.

4 *Decisiveness*

Ability to recognize when a decision is required (disregarding the quality of the decision) and to act quickly.

5 *Leadership*

Ability to get others involved in solving problems; ability to recognize when a group requires direction, to interact with a group effectively and to guide them to the accomplishment of a task.

6 *Sensitivity*

Ability to perceive the needs, concerns and personal problems of others; skill in resolving conflicts; tact in dealing with persons from different backgrounds; ability to deal effectively with people concerning emotional issues; knowing what information to communicate and to whom.

7 *Range of interests*

Competence to discuss a variety of subjects – educational, political, current events, economic, etc.; desire actively to participate in events.

8 *Personal motivation*

Need to achieve in all activities attempted; evidence that work is important to personal satisfaction; ability to be self-policing.

9 *Educational values*

Possession of a well-reasoned educational philosophy; receptiveness to new ideas and change.

10 *Stress tolerance*

Ability to perform under pressure and during opposition; ability to think on one's feet.

11 *Oral communication*

Ability to make a clear oral presentation of facts or ideas.

12 *Written communication*

Ability to express ideas clearly in writing; to write appropriately for different audiences – students, teachers, parents, *et al.*

National Association of Secondary School Principals (NASSP)
Reston, VA
22091–1537
USA

The National Educational Assessment Centre (NEAC)
Competencies (from NEAC 1995)

The NEAC assesses 12 competencies, which experience and research have proved, are necessary for successful senior management in schools. They are divided into four groups – administrative, interpersonal, communicative and personal breadth competencies.

Administrative Competencies

Problem analysis

Ability to seek out relevant data (verbal and numerical) and analyze information to determine the important elements of a problem situation; to search for information with a purpose; to identify potential organizational problems and opportunities associated with changing situations outside school (including community and governmental pressures).

Judgment

Ability to reach logical conclusions and make high quality decisions based on available information; to identify educational needs and to set priorities both short term and longer term (strategic thinking); to evaluate written communications critically and show caution where necessary. Willingness to take calculated risks.

Organizational ability

Ability to plan and schedule effectively; to delegate appropriately; to perceive longer term changes and to prepare for them; to implement change successfully.

Decisiveness

Ability to recognize when a decision is required (disregarding the quality of the decision) and to act upon it.

Interpersonal Competencies

Leadership

Ability to motivate others in addressing issues and involve them in solving problems; to recognize when direction is required and to give guidance towards the accomplishment of a task; to generate new ideas; to secure general acceptance of ideas after modifying them if necessary. Willingness to engage in proactive behaviour and seize opportunities to project a personal view.

Sensitivity

Ability to perceive needs, concerns and problems from differing viewpoints; to value the contribution of others; to display tact in dealing with people with different backgrounds and outlooks; to deal effectively with people concerning emotional issues; to cope with aggression. Knowing what information to communicate and to whom.

Stress tolerance

Ability to perform under pressure; to cope with the necessary efforts to overcome obstacles and/or perform tasks.

Communicative Competencies

Oral communication

Ability to make clear oral presentation of facts or ideas both, one to one, in small groups and to large audiences.

Written communication

Ability to express ideas clearly in writing; to write appropriately for different audiences – students, teachers, parents *et al.*

Personal Breadth Competencies

Range of interests

Ability to discuss a variety of subjects; educational, political, topical, economic and religious etc. Desire to participate actively in events both on and off the job.

Personal motivation

Need to achieve in all activities attempted. Evidence that work is important to personal satisfaction. Evidence of continuing action to improve personal capability. Ability to be self-evaluating.

Educational values

Possession and demonstration of well-reasoned educational philosophy and an understanding of current educational issues. Skill in projecting a personal educational vision.

**The Teacher Training Agency 'Headlamp' Competencies
(from the TTA 1995): Managerial Tasks and Abilities**

Each headteacher's training programme will need to focus on one or more of a
range of leadership and management *tasks* drawn from the following:

- defining the aims and objectives of the school;
- developing, implementing, monitoring and reviewing policies for all aspects
  of the school, including the curriculum, assessment, classroom organization
  and management, teaching approaches and pupil support;
- planning and managing resource provision;
- assessing and reviewing standards of pupils' achievements and the quality
  of teaching and learning;
- selecting and managing staff, and appraising their performance;
- liaising with parents, the local community and other organizations and
  institutions.

In addition, each headteacher's training programme will need to focus on one or
more of a range of leadership and management *abilities*, including the ability to:

- give a clear sense of direction and purpose in order to achieve the school's
  mission and inspire staff and pupils alike;
- anticipate problems, make judgments and take decisions;
- adapt to changing circumstances and new ideas;
- solve problems;
- negotiate, delegate, consult and coordinate the efforts of others;
- follow through and pursue policies to implementation and monitor and
  review their effectiveness in practice;
- understand and keep up-to-date with current educational and management
  issues and identify their relevance to the school;
- communicate effectively with staff at all levels, pupils, parents, governors
  and the wider community.

The School Management South Competencies (from School Management South 1992): An Overview of the Key Purpose, Key Roles and Units of Competence for School Management

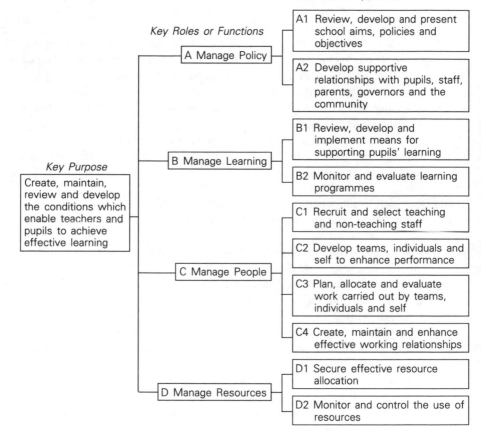

(For further information see Earley 1992).

The Management Charter Initiative (MCI): Personal Effectiveness Model (from MCI 1990)

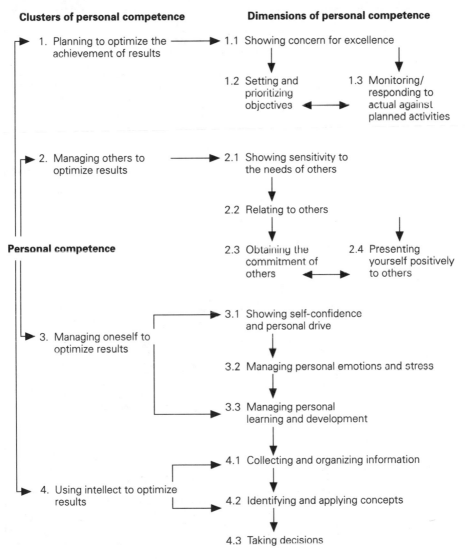

Clusters of personal competence

Dimensions of personal competence

1. Planning to optimize the achievement of results

1.1 Showing concern for excellence

1.2 Setting and prioritizing objectives

1.3 Monitoring/responding to actual against planned activities

2. Managing others to optimize results

2.1 Showing sensitivity to the needs of others

2.2 Relating to others

Personal competence

2.3 Obtaining the commitment of others

2.4 Presenting yourself positively to others

3. Managing oneself to optimize results

3.1 Showing self-confidence and personal drive

3.2 Managing personal emotions and stress

3.3 Managing personal learning and development

4. Using intellect to optimize results

4.1 Collecting and organizing information

4.2 Identifying and applying concepts

4.3 Taking decisions

(For further information see MCI 1990).

Saville and Holdsworth's Core Competency Model: the Inventory of Management Competencies (from Saville and Holdsworth 1993b)

Area	Competency	Definition
COMMERCIAL and PROFESSIONAL	Commercial	Understands and applies commercial and financial principles. Views issues in terms of costs, profits, markets and added value.
	Expert	Understands technical or professional aspects of work and continually maintains technical knowledge.
REASONING AREAS	Analytical	Analyzes issues and breaks them down into their component parts. Makes systematic and rational judgments based on relevant information.
	Innovative	Creates new and imaginative approaches to work-related issues. Identifies fresh approaches and shows a willingness to question traditional assumptions.
	Strategic	Demonstrates a broad-based view of issues, events and activities and a perception of their longer term impact or wider implications.
	Organized	Organizes and schedules events, activities and resources. Sets up and monitors timescales and plans.
	Decisive	Demonstrates a readiness to make decisions, take the initiative and originate action.
INTERPERSONAL QUALITIES	Articulate	Speaks clearly, fluently and in a compelling manner to both individuals and groups.
	Literate	Writes in a clear and concise manner, using appropriate grammar, style and language for the reader.
	Supportive	Interacts with others in a sensitive and effective way. Respects and works well with others.
	Persuasive	Influences, convinces or impresses others in a way that results in acceptance, agreement or behaviour change.
	Coordinating	Motivates and empowers individuals and teams in order to reach organizational goals.
PERSONAL QUALITIES	Quality-driven	Shows awareness of goals and standards. Follows through to ensure that quality and productivity standards are met.
	Flexible	Successfully adapts to changing demands and conditions.
	Resilient	Maintains effective work behaviour in the face of set-backs or pressure. Remains calm, stable and in control of themselves.
	Motivated	Commits self to work hard towards goals. Shows enthusiasm and career commitment.

The McBer/Boyatzis Competencies: (from Boyatzis 1982 and Boak 1991)

'Actual' competencies – distinguishing the superior from the average manager:

- *efficiency orientation* – concern with doing something better;
- *proactivity* – disposition toward initiating activity;
- *concern with impact* – concern with the symbols and uses of power;
- *diagnostic use of concepts* – use of previously held concepts to explain and interpret situations;
- *managing group process* – ability to stimulate others to work effectively in a group setting;
- *use of socialized power* – use of influence to build alliances, networks, or coalitions;
- *self-confidence* – ability consistently to display decisiveness or presence;
- *conceptualization* – use of new concepts to identify a pattern in an assortment of information;
- *self-control* – ability to inhibit personal needs;
- *stamina and adaptability* – the energy to sustain long hours of work and the flexibility to adapt to changes;
- *perceptual objectivity* – ability to be relatively objective;
- *use of oral presentations* – ability to make effective oral presentations to others.

'Threshold' competencies – essential to doing the job but not related to 'superior' performance:

- *use of unilateral power* – use of forms of influence;
- *developing others* – ability to provide performance feedback;
- *spontaneity* – ability to express oneself freely and easily;
- *accurate self-assessment* – realistic and grounded view of oneself;
- *positive regard* – ability to express a positive belief in others;
- *logical thought* – order events in a causal sequence;
- *specialized knowledge* – possession and mastery of specialized knowledge relevant to the job.

Appendix 6

Headteachers' Management Competencies: Indicative Pro Forma for a Self-Evaluation Based Management Development Exercise

Headteacher Management Competencies

Competence Areas	*Competencies*
Professional and technical knowledge	Professional knowledge Technical knowledge
The planning and administrative process	Analyzing Planning Directional leadership
Dealing with people	Sensitivity Motivating Evaluating
Managing the political environment	Political ability Persuading and negotiating
Personal skills	Commitment and values Reasoning and judgment Self-awareness and development Projecting a favourable image and communicating

Headteacher Management Competencies

This form can help you, first, to identify areas of your present job, or of your next job if you prefer, where you may be keen to build upon your existing skills, or second, where you feel some training and development would help improve a competence at present not one of your strengths.

You should complete the exercise (self-evaluation pages), and then using the pro forma at the end identify, then prioritize your skills or development requirements.

It is always more useful if you could ask a colleague to act as a critical friend and agree with you the ratings you have made.

Instructions for the Self-Evaluation Exercise

First, will you rate your performance for each competence using the following criteria:

(1) Does not match specification
(2) Matches specification in some respects but some important omissions
(3) Matches specification fairly well but has weaknesses in a few aspects
(4) Fully matches specification with no doubt at all.

Will you then provide some evidence or justification for each of your evaluations.

Please remember, we do not expect anyone to be good at everything.

Second, will you please indicate your personal interest in each competence using the rating scale below:

This competence is:	*Rating*
a particularly uninteresting area for me	1
an area of low interest for me	2
an area of moderate interest for me	3
a particularly interesting area for me	4

The pro forma gives an indication of the steps you should follow. If you require more space for your responses, then please use as many sheets of paper as you wish.

Self-Evaluation

	Performance Rating (1–4)	Interest Rating (1–4)

1 Professional and Technical Knowledge

Professional knowledge

Exercises knowledge of matters appertaining to the management of the curricular, instructional, pedagogic, and welfare processes to give firm educational leadership to the school and community.

Please circle

1 2 3 4

Please circle

1 2 3 4

Evidence of:

something which went well

_____

_____

something which went less well

_____

_____

Technical knowledge

Has knowledge of, and can deal efficiently with, the legal, statutory, financial, and budgetary processes currently impinging upon the school.

Please circle

1 2 3 4

Please circle

1 2 3 4

Evidence of:

something which went well

_____

_____

something which went less well

_____

_____

	Performance Rating (1–4)	Interest Rating (1–4)

2 *The Planning and Administrative Process*

Analyzing

Is able to analyze contextual factors, diagnose difficulties, and seek necessary information in order to inform vision, generate and evaluate alternatives for action, and to provide the basis for future planning.

Please circle 1 2 3 4   Please circle 1 2 3 4

Evidence of:

something which went well

_____

_____

something which went less well

_____

_____

Planning

Uses vision and a future orientation to develop long term goals and strategies, as well as planning to meet immediate problems and needs. Initiates and develops planning procedures for curriculum, community, staff, pupils, and budgetary matters.

Please circle 1 2 3 4   Please circle 1 2 3 4

Evidence of:

something which went well

_____

_____

something which went less well

_____

_____

	Performance Rating (1–4)	**Interest Rating (1–4)**

Directional leadership

Sets standards and gives direction to the school. Makes decisions, and devises and implements administrative systems for organizing human and other resources. Brings tasks successfully to completion by delegation and through appropriate use of time and attention to detail.

Please circle   Please circle

1 2 3 4   1 2 3 4

Evidence of:

something which went well

_____

_____

something which went less well

_____

_____

3 Dealing with People

Sensitivity

Is accessible, sensitive, and uses tact and diplomacy in helping pupils, parents, staff, and governors.

Please circle   Please circle

1 2 3 4   1 2 3 4

Evidence of:

something which went well

_____

_____

something which went less well

_____

_____

	Performance Rating (1–4)	Interest Rating (1–4)

Motivating

Motivates and mobilizes others by promoting an ethos of excellence, individual and team development, and collaborative decision making. Provides support and resources to maximize personal and professional development.

Please circle   Please circle

1 2 3 4   1 2 3 4

Evidence of:

something which went well

_____

_____

something which went less well

_____

_____

Evaluating

Promotes confidence amongst staff and pupils by setting up systems to enable monitoring and evaluating of their work and progress. Appraises staff strengths and needs for purposes of personal development and recruitment, retention, and promotion.

Please circle   Please circle

1 2 3 4   1 2 3 4

Evidence of:

something which went well

_____

_____

something which went less well

_____

_____

	Performance Rating (1–4)	**Interest Rating (1–4)**

4 Managing the Political Environment

Political ability

Is politically adept, can develop and maintain a network of contacts, and is aware of own relationship to the wider political environment. Generates support amongst stakeholders for the school.

Please circle   Please circle

1 2 3 4   1 2 3 4

Evidence of:

something which went well

_____

_____

something which went less well

_____

_____

Persuading and negotiating

Is persuasive and negotiates with various interest groups, if necessary being tough minded and firm in dealing with conflicts in order to achieve a successful outcome.

Please circle   Please circle

1 2 3 4   1 2 3 4

Evidence of:

something which went well

_____

_____

something which went less well

_____

_____

	Performance Rating (1–4)	Interest Rating (1–4)

5 Personal Skills and Self-Management

Commitment and values

Displays commitment to the school through strength of personal beliefs, by own energy and enthusiasm and by maintaining own morale.	Please circle 1 2 3 4	Please circle 1 2 3 4

Evidence of:

something which went well

_____
_____

something which went less well

_____
_____

Reasoning and judgment

Is able to reason logically with verbal, written, and numerical data, critically evaluate information received, and exercise judgment in making decisions and solving problems.	Please circle 1 2 3 4	Please circle 1 2 3 4

Evidence of:

something which went well

_____
_____

something which went less well

_____
_____

Self-awareness and development

In recognizing the need for continuous personal and professional development, keeps abreast of new educational developments, actively monitors own performance, and has wider interests outside the school. Is able to respond to change by generating ideas for organizational renewal.	Please circle 1 2 3 4	Please circle 1 2 3 4

	Performance Rating (1–4)	Interest Rating (1–4)

Evidence of:

something which went well

_____

_____

something which went less well

_____

_____

Projecting a favourable image and communicating

Establishes visibility and credibility for school by confidently projecting the school and its goals. Communicates effectively both orally and in writing, even when under pressure, adapting style according to the audience.	Please circle 1 2 3 4	Please circle 1 2 3 4

Evidence of:

something which went well

_____

_____

something which went less well

_____

_____

When you are prioritizing your development needs (your importance rating), note:

- your 'interest rating score' as a likely indicator of your own motivation;
- the extent to which your development priorities are in step with the school development plans;
- whether the training/development can be on the job;
- self-monitored; or
- that you might need to go outside of the school to undertake training with a training organization, or with consultants, or on an award-bearing programme in higher education.

You must be quite clear as to how you intend to evaluate your progress.

Integration Pro Forma: Management Competencies Joint Performance Ratings

	Competence	Performance Rating	Importance Rating
1	Professional knowledge	1 2 3 4	
2	Technical knowledge	1 2 3 4	
3	Analyzing	1 2 3 4	
4	Planning	1 2 3 4	
5	Directional leadership	1 2 3 4	
6	Sensitivity	1 2 3 4	
7	Motivating	1 2 3 4	
8	Evaluating	1 2 3 4	
9	Political ability	1 2 3 4	
10	Persuading and negotiating	1 2 3 4	
11	Commitment and values	1 2 3 4	
12	Reasoning and judgment	1 2 3 4	
13	Self-awareness and development	1 2 3 4	
14	Projecting a favourable image and communicating	1 2 3 4	

Agreed Development Priorities Training and Development Action Plan

Priority 1

Action to be taken:

_____

_____

_____

_____

Standard to be achieved and indicative evidence to be produced:

_____

_____

_____

_____

Proposed review and date:

_____

_____

_____

_____

Follow-up action required:

_____

_____

_____

_____

Then agree Priority 2, etc.

© Education Management Research Group
University of East London
East London Business School
Duncan House
High Street
London E15 2JB

Index